SEEKING
JOHN
CAMPBELL

To Dave
with best wishes
John Daffurn
_7.2.15_

SEEKING
JOHN
CAMPBELL

Finding pioneers &
patriots in the pampas

JOHN DAFFURN

Eptex

First published in Great Britain by Eptex in 2015
Eptex
Litton House, Saville Road
Peterborough, PE3 7PR

Copyright © John Daffurn 2015

A CIP catalogue record for this book is available
from the British Library.

ISBN 978-0-9931479-0-6

Typeset in Fairfield by
Chandler Book Design

Printed in Great Britain by
Print-On-Demand Worldwide

Cover Art—Image of pampas:
© istockphoto.com/PPAMPicture.
John Burnet Campbell: courtesy of King's College
London, Foyle Special Collections Library. John Otto
Campbell: courtesy of A. Campbell. John Argentine
Campbell: courtesy of John A. Campbell.

Cover Design by John Daffurn and
Chandler Book Design

To the families of cousins

Major R. M. Campbell MC

and

Oberleutnant M. A. d. Res. H. Philippi DKIG

who were both killed in action
in the autumn of 1944

CONTENTS

Illustrations

Unless otherwise stated the images listed below are being used with the kind permission of the various Philippi and Campbell families or are provided by the author.

1. Hugh Robson. © Graeme Wall, 2004–2014
2. *Symmetry*. From *Book of the Bazaar* (Buenos Aires, 1927). Courtesy of Colecciones Especiales y Archivos de la Universidad de San Andres: Argentina
3. Estancia la Adela, c. 1870. Photograph by James Niven, Colecciones Especiales y Archivos de la Universidad de San Andres: Argentina
4. Estancia La Juanita, 2014. Formerly Estancia La Adela
5. Original building at Estancia La Corona
6. John Campbell senior. Courtesy of John A. Campbell
7. John Argentine (left) and Roderick Campbell. Courtesy of John A. Campbell
8. John Burnet Campbell, c. 1918. From 'Special Peace Number' Revista Del Río de La Plata (1919). Courtesy of King's College London, Foyle Special Collections Library
9. Estancia La Corona, 2014

10. Alexander David in 1760. From R. Philippi, private chronicle of the Philippi family, Repro Braunschweigisches Landesmuseum, Niedersächsische Landesmuseen Braunschweig, I. Simon

11. Hermann Philippi

12. Otto Ernst Philippi

13. Otto Heinrich Philippi. Courtesy of Verena Auffermann

14. Mary Campbell Philippi (née Gibson)

15. 'Jock', 2nd Lt J. Campbell, East Yorkshire Militia Regiment c. 1902

16. Aimee Dorothy Campbell (née Philips)

17. Estancia Los Dos Hermanos, c. 1906

18. Dorothy Campbell and her cartoon 'Doly-Booboo'

19. Cartoon of 'Doly-Booboo' with groom Elias

20. 'Jock', 2nd Lt J. Campbell, Royal Field Artillery, c. 1915

21. John Argentine, 2nd Lt J. A. Campbell, 6th Inniskilling Dragoons, c. 1915. Courtesy of John A. Campbell

22. Pond Cottage, Crawley Court Estate. Trish Steel, 'Pond Cottage, Crawley' 25 February 2007, Geograph, Creative Commons Attribution

23. Section of illustration from A Tale of Inca Times by Jock Campbell, 1902. Courtesy of Verena Auffermann

24. Richard Philippi. Courtesy of Verena Auffermann

25. Herbert Philippi. Courtesy of Verena Auffermann

26. Roderick Campbell, 2nd Lt R. Campbell, 1st Battalion Black Watch. Courtesy of John A. Campbell

27. Tony Campbell. Photograph of sketch by Augustus John, London, 1944. Courtesy of John A. Campbell

28. Michael Campbell, Major R. M. Campbell MC, 1st Battalion Black Watch

29. John Campbell's signature on Isabel's Argentine birth certificate (top) and on 1911 UK Census

30. Isabel Campbell, c. 1945

Acknowledgements

As I had never planned to write a book, it is a rather odd that I now find myself penning an acknowledgments section. When I started this project, as an exercise in genealogical research, my family humoured me as I spent hours in front of my computer, following any and every lead that might take me a step forward in the process. As the story unfolded their ambivalence changed to interest and I was grateful for their support, which kept me going.

I was also boosted by the positive responses I received from total strangers, whether website hosts, web forum contributors, librarians, archivists or authors. In particular I must thank the descendants of the families whom I have written about. All were surprised when I contacted them and many were initially suspicious of my overtures. But, invariably, information to help me was forthcoming, and in many cases I was able to share the most private of letters and documents in their possession.

Others who have contributed and made my task easier include Archibald John Campbell (sadly deceased),

Eugenia Cruset, Juan Delius, Eleanor Leese, Reinhard Philippi, Nicky Stephen, and Graeme Wall.

Finally, a heartfelt thanks to those who made my visit to Argentina so memorable and completed my journey of discovery: John and Hilda Campbell, Rodolfo Antonio Casen, Pamela Cortina, Carlos Foglia, Santiago Garrido, Alastair Henderson, Silvana Piga, Fany Romagnoli, Josefina Badano Sola, and Natalia Westberg.

Monetary Values

Pound Sterling values have been converted using the National Archive currency converter until 2005 and the Retail Price Index (RPI) from 2005 to 2014.

Argentine pesos were converted to US dollars and then to Pounds Sterling; then to present day value as above.

German Marks were converted to gold ozs; then to US dollars and from US dollars to Pound Sterling; then to present day value as above.

Genealogy charts

Genealogy of
John Burnet Campbell

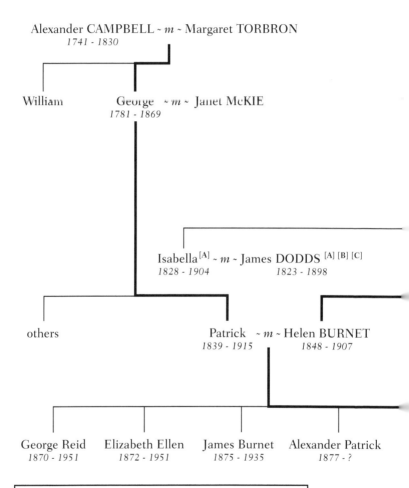

Alexander CAMPBELL ~ *m* ~ Margaret TORBRON
1741 - 1830

William   George ~ *m* ~ Janet McKIE
                           1781 - 1869

Isabella [A] ~ *m* ~ James DODDS [A] [B] [C]
1828 - 1904   *1823 - 1898*

others   Patrick ~ *m* ~ Helen BURNET
                          1839 - 1915   *1848 - 1907*

George Reid   Elizabeth Ellen   James Burnet   Alexander Patrick
1870 - 1951   *1872 - 1951*   *1875 - 1935*   *1877 - ?*

NOTES:
[A] Sailed to Argentina in 1844 on the *Prince of Wales*
[B] Author of *Records of Scottish Settlers*
[C] Original joint owners of Estancia La Adela

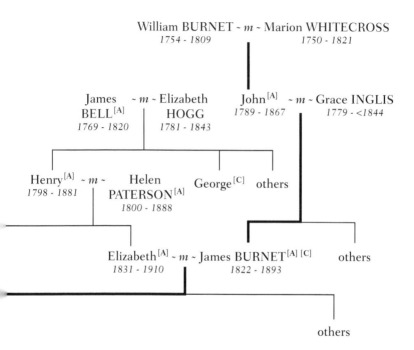

William BURNET ~ *m* ~ Marion WHITECROSS
1754 - 1809   1750 - 1821

James   ~ *m* ~ Elizabeth   John[A]   ~ *m* ~ Grace INGLIS
BELL[A]   HOGG   1789 - 1867   1779 - <1844
1769 - 1820   1781 - 1843

Henry[A] ~ *m* ~   Helen   George[C]   others
1798 - 1881   PATERSON[A]
                     1800 - 1888

Elizabeth[A] ~ *m* ~ James BURNET[A] [C]   others
1831 - 1910   1822 - 1893

                                        others

John Burnet ~ *m* ~ Maria Carmen   William Angus
CAMPBELL   BROWNE   1882 - 1924
1879 - ?

Genealogy of
John Argentine Campbell

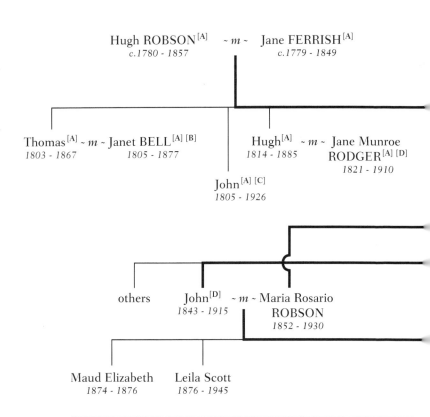

Hugh ROBSON[A] ~ *m* ~ Jane FERRISH[A]
c.1780 - 1857   c.1779 - 1849

Thomas[A] ~ *m* ~ Janet BELL[A] [B]
1803 - 1867   1805 - 1877

Hugh[A] ~ *m* ~ Jane Munroe
1814 - 1885   RODGER[A] [D]
1821 - 1910

John[A] [C]
1805 - 1926

others   John[D] ~ *m* ~ Maria Rosario
1843 - 1915   ROBSON
1852 - 1930

Maud Elizabeth   Leila Scott
1874 - 1876   1876 - 1945

NOTES:
[A] Immigrants on the *Symmetry*
[B] Sister of Henry Bell (see John Burnet Campbell genealogy)
[C] Killed at Monte Grande by marauding soldiers
[D] Founders of the Hurlingham Club, Buenos Aires
[E] Best polo player, of his era, in Argentina

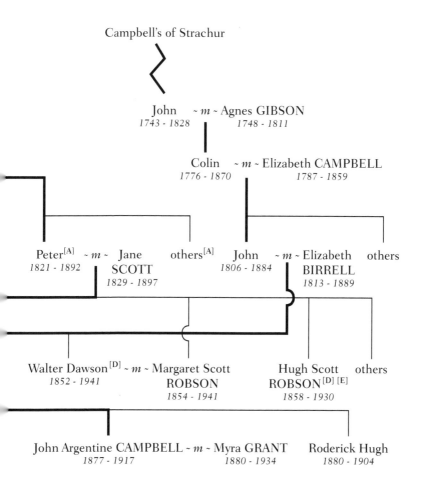

Campbell's of Strachur

John ~ *m* ~ Agnes GIBSON
1743 - 1828   1748 - 1811

Colin ~ *m* ~ Elizabeth CAMPBELL
1776 - 1870   1787 - 1859

Peter[A] ~ *m* ~ Jane   others[A]   John   ~ *m* ~ Elizabeth   others
1821 - 1892   SCOTT   1806 - 1884   BIRRELL
                     1829 - 1897   1813 - 1889

Walter Dawson[D] ~ *m* ~ Margaret Scott   Hugh Scott   others
1852 - 1941   ROBSON   ROBSON[D] [E]
                        1854 - 1941   1858 - 1930

John Argentine CAMPBELL ~ *m* ~ Myra GRANT   Roderick Hugh
1877 - 1917   1880 - 1934   1880 - 1904

Genealogy of
John Otto Campbell

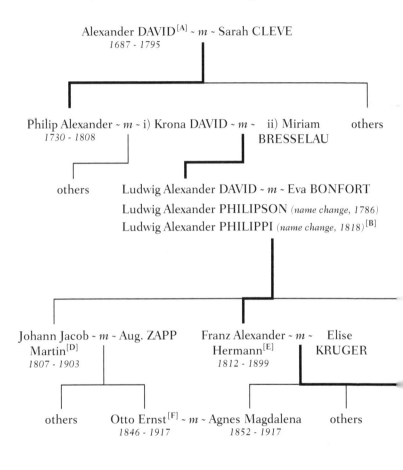

Alexander DAVID[A] ~ *m* ~ Sarah CLEVE
1687 - 1795

Philip Alexander ~ *m* ~ i) Krona DAVID ~ *m* ~   ii) Miriam   others
1730 - 1808   BRESSELAU

others   Ludwig Alexander DAVID ~ *m* ~ Eva BONFORT
Ludwig Alexander PHILIPSON *(name change, 1786)*
Ludwig Alexander PHILIPPI *(name change, 1818)*[B]

Johann Jacob ~ *m* ~ Aug. ZAPP   Franz Alexander ~ *m* ~   Elise
Martin[D]   Hermann[E]   KRUGER
1807 - 1903   *1812 - 1899*

others   Otto Ernst[F] ~ *m* ~ Agnes Magdalena   others
1846 - 1917   *1852 - 1917*

Otto Campbell PHILIPPI ~ *m* ~ Aimee Dorothy PHILIPS
John Otto CAMPBELL   *1879 - 1970*
(name change, 1902)
1880 - 1938

NOTES:
[A] Court Jew to Dukes of Brunswick
[B] Conversion to Lutheranism in 1813
[C] Founded Leith shipping company in 1797
[D] Theologian and Rector at Solingen
[E] Head of family bank J. Magnus & Co
[F] Director of J.P.Coats

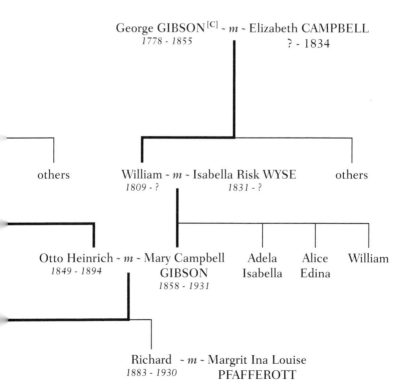

George GIBSON[C] ~ *m* ~ Elizabeth CAMPBELL
1778 - 1855   ? - 1834

others   William ~ *m* ~ Isabella Risk WYSE   others
                1809 - ?   *1831 - ?*

Otto Heinrich ~ *m* ~ Mary Campbell   Adela   Alice   William
1849 - 1894   GIBSON   Isabella   Edina
                          1858 - 1931

Richard ~ *m* ~ Margrit Ina Louise
1883 - 1930   PFAFFEROTT

Prologue

Curiosity is lying in wait for every secret
Ralph Waldo Emerson

At the end of 1995, sixty-eight-year-old Isabel Greig returned to Stone House, her home in the market town of Petworth, West Sussex, after enjoying a quiet visit with an old schoolfriend in Bath. It had been her first Christmas without her husband, Ian, who had died a couple of months earlier after a battle with cancer. Widowed after almost forty years of marriage, Isabel was lost.

Isabel was a striking woman, caring and unselfish and not without a sense of fun in happier times. She received fulsome support from her neighbours following the death of her beloved Ian, and when she returned after Christmas she telephoned a friend, who lived in a cottage opposite, but was persuaded not to visit her that evening as she was suffering from flu. The country was in the grip of the coldest winter for fourteen years and the following morning Isabel woke to a dusting of snow. Later that day, after light rain had washed the snow away, Isabel ventured out, but within yards of her home, slipped on black ice and fell to the ground, giving herself a hefty knock to the back of her head.

A passing policeman comforted her and a neighbour took her in for a soothing cup of tea. Isabel regained her composure and, typically not wishing to make a fuss, assured everybody that she was fine. She returned to her house, saying that she would take it easy for the rest of the day. Her friend across the road, still recovering from influenza and unaware of Isabel's fall, was not surprised that she hadn't called that day, expecting her to be enjoying the company of those in better health.

When Isabel's neighbour knocked on her door the following morning, New Year's Eve 1995, there was no response. Eventually, the police were called, the door was forced and on entering the house they found the lifeless Isabel in her bed. She had passed away during the night from what was later diagnosed as a brain haemorrhage. The coroner recorded a verdict of accidental death.

Fifteen years later, I was scanning the UK government's list of estates unclaimed by relatives, which is held by the Treasury Solicitor. Each week their Bona Vacantia department add new estates and probate genealogists race to find potential heirs and help them to claim their money in return for a commission. Genealogy has been of interest to me for more than forty years and I had been surprised to discover that, apart from the weekly release, more than ten thousand other estates, going back thirty years, remained unclaimed. Why were these cases unresolved? Why had professional heir-hunters failed to unlock their secrets? Many of the cases would have been of little value and discarded as unprofitable at a time, pre-2007, when the values of the estates were published. Others must have been too difficult, or costly, to solve.

With available time and a thirst for problem-solving, I considered finding out why those who had tried to solve the cases had failed. It would be an intellectual challenge, a genealogical jigsaw puzzle that, even if it ended in failure, would enhance my ancestry research skills. My curiosity got the better of me and I searched the list of unsolved cases to pluck one out for initial research, assuming that the heir-hunting roadblock would quickly become apparent.

My action was no more sophisticated than scrolling the list to the Gs and sticking an imaginary pin on the computer screen. I was drawn to a female name and her details indicated that she may be a prime candidate for my research. Almost fifteen years had elapsed since her death, providing the heir-hunters with plenty of time to make their initial investigations into the case, yet it remained open. Another factor was that she was one of a small percentage of persons listed with three given names: always an additional aid in genealogical research. Furthermore, the third given name appeared to be a maiden or family name, providing additional clues for the researcher. Maria Isabel Pemberton Greig, who died at Petworth, Sussex, on 31 December 1995, was to be my test case.

Isabel was on the Bona Vacantia list because she had died before making a will: something her friends had urged her to do after the death of her husband in October 1995. She had no children and since her death none of the probate researchers had managed to locate any living heirs. Under UK intestacy rules Isabel's parents or siblings, if they could be identified, became the next potential beneficiaries.

It did not take long for me to discover, from a simple internet search, that Isabel had become a naturalised British citizen in 1951, and that she had been born in Argentina. From another source I found her marriage record, and a copy of her marriage certificate provided details of her father, John Campbell, a rancher. Finding this information so quickly, in the summer of 2010, was exhilarating, but I still needed to trace her mother. Internet genealogical databases have flourished in the last twenty years and, besides the bread-and-butter birth, marriage and death registers, commercial companies have digitised many other records, including passenger lists collected by the British Board of Trade and held at the National Archives. From the information I had already found, I knew that Isabel must have travelled to the UK at a date prior to 1951.

By searching the Incoming Passenger Lists to the UK, I found, after several false starts, a record for Mary Isabel Campbell, born in 1927 and travelling in 1929. The original document also included her destination address. As a two-year-old, Isabel could not have travelled alone, but the adjacent entries did not provide a clue to her guardian. Further down the page, with passengers listed in alphabetical order, the name Pemberton jumped from the screen. Gladys Pemberton had provided the same destination address and my immediate assumption was that she was the mother of (the possibly illegitimate) Isabel.

Such success in a matter of days was surprising, but it was a false dawn. Armed with the names of those whom I believed to be Isabel's parents, I embarked upon a detailed search to unlock the genealogy of both. The search for her father was difficult, as he had been living in Argentina, a Spanish-speaking country, which left me with little capability for online research. Taking the blunderbuss approach, I posted messages on internet genealogy forums, resulting in quite remarkable and detailed responses. Before long I had more Argentine-based John Campbells than I knew what to do with, and had entered into detailed dialogues with other Campbell researchers in Australia, France, Germany and the UK. Months passed as my Campbell candidates, for one reason or another, were cast aside and my attention became focussed on three in particular.

John Argentine Campbell, John Burnet Campbell and John Otto Campbell had much in common. All had been born on, or had owned, *estancias* (ranches). They were fit and strong and were either good sports- or horsemen. More remarkably, even though not required to do so, either they or their sons returned to the UK to fight in WWI and WWII. Finally, they were all born within three years of each other, were of an age to have fathered Isabel and were from privileged backgrounds.

My curiosity drove me to try and unlock the secrets of Isabel's ancestry, but, in the process, I uncovered the pioneering and patriotic lives of the families of these John Campbells. I became engrossed in their histories, their families' migrations to the Argentine, and their involvement in the social and sporting history of Argentina.

1

Migration to Argentina

*One secret of success in life is for a man to be
ready for his opportunity when it comes.*

Benjamin Disraeli

The three John Campbells differed in one important
way. One of them had chosen to emigrate to
Argentina as a young man, whereas the two others
had been born there, descendants of migrants, who decades
before had forsaken Scotland in search of a better life.
Their ancestors had been part of a wave of mass migration,
previously unseen outside of the USA, which emanated from
the formation of Argentina as an independent state.

Early in the nineteenth century, Rio de la Plata, an area
covering Uruguay, Paraguay and present-day Argentina, was
ruled as a viceroyalty from Spain, a situation which had
remained unchanged for almost three hundred years. The
criollo population (those locally born of Spanish descent)
were becoming ever more frustrated at being governed by
a distant monarch, and when in May 1810 news arrived in

Buenos Ayres that Napoleon I had deposed their king and religious leader, they seized their chance for change. On 25 May, a date that remains pre-eminent in Argentine history, the *Primera Junta*, or First Assembly, was established and, despite swearing its allegiance to the King of Spain, it immediately removed the viceroy from power.

A few years later, difficult negotiations with Spain for self-determination failed and in 1816 the thirty or so deputies of the Argentine National Assembly travelled from across the country to the foothills of the towering Aconquija mountains, more than eight hundred miles north-west of Buenos Ayres. There, over a couple of months in a rented house in San Miguel de Tucumán, they developed and eventually signed a declaration of independence for a new state that would become Argentina. It also signified the start of social, cultural and political change that would harness immigration and change the country forever.

Bernardino Rivadavia, the son of a Spanish lawyer and a former Junta member, who had been unsuccessful in the independence discussions with Spain, had remained in Europe, not returning until 1821, when he was appointed secretary to the government. His time away from Argentina had not been wasted. Impressed by the culture and urban development in Europe, especially in Paris, he set about improving Buenos Ayres and creating what would become known, towards the end of the century, as the Paris of Latin America. Universities, boulevards and museums were all part of his plan, yet it was his encouragement of immigration and colonisation which would have a lasting national effect. In 1823 he was granted executive power to support colonisation and the next year Rivadavia set up the Immigration Commission, which had the power to contract with those wishing to begin a new life in Argentina.

It was via this newly formed commission that the Scottish brothers William and John Parish Robertson, who were successful merchants in Buenos Ayres, approached the government with a plan to create a colony of Scots in the Argentine. The Robertsons' commercial success was based upon trading in hides and setting up profitable mercantile connections with England and Scotland, following a trip by John to the British Isles in 1817. When he returned to Scotland, in 1824, to recruit his immigrants, it was on his own vessel, carrying a £100,000 (c. £6m) fortune.[1] In John's absence his brother, William, negotiated the contract for the colony, including the provision of land, which was ratified by Rivadavia in March 1824.[2]

In the first half of the nineteenth century, the economy of Scotland was in a parlous state. Highland landowners forcefully evicted tenants who could not pay their way, clearing the crofters' land to make way for more-profitable sheep-farming. Most of those removed refused to transfer to the Scottish lowlands and many were instead forced to emigrate. The lowland residents did not escape unemployment or economic depression either, but in their case migration was a more voluntary option, hopefully providing themselves and their families with a better chance to advance in life. It was from this catchment of willing potential émigrés that John Parish Robertson found the future colonists of Monte Grande.

One of his key recruits was William Grierson, a farmer from Mouswald, Dumfriesshire, whose accounting records with the Robertsons survive in print.[3] From these records, although individuals are identified only by initials, it is possible to deduce which farm labourers and servants Grierson chose, and/or convinced, to travel with him. Amongst these was Hugh Robson, a ploughman with strong chiselled features who may have worked for the Grierson family.

Hugh Robson

Hugh lived with his family in Torthorwald, less than four miles from where Grierson was born, and had spent his working life within seven miles of this village. Yet, in a continual search for employment, he was forced to move from farm to farm. From Kirkmichael, his place of birth, above the valley of the meandering Water of Ae; to Tinwald, with sweeping views of the undulating hills south to Dumfries and finally to Torthorwald, overlooked by the ruins of its fourteenth-century castle. It was a hard yet satisfying outdoor life in the summer, but a harsh and unrelenting winter struggle on the unprotected arable landscape.

This, together with an uncertain income to care for his large family and little hope of any improvement in the future, must have made emigrating an easy choice.

At the end of April 1825, Hugh and his family, under the patronage of Grierson, headed to Edinburgh by stagecoach. It seems that Grierson, as a goodwill gesture, paid Robson, three other ploughmen and two servant girls a half-year's salary in advance of sailing to the Argentine. In addition, Grierson also bore the cost of travel to Edinburgh and three weeks' accommodation for Robson's family as they waited close to the port of Leith.[4]

On the other side of Scotland, in East Lothian, Thomas Bell, a twenty-seven-year-old bachelor and farm bailiff, was also tempted by the offer of a new and exciting life on the other side of the world. Thomas was the eldest son of James Bell, a ploughman from East Barns, only a few miles from the east coast of Scotland and exposed to the elements of the North Sea. He would be one of many from a concentrated area, within a triangle drawn from Haddington, North Berwick and Cockburnspath, to settle in Argentina over the next quarter of a century.

By the middle of May, most of Robertson's recruits: farmers, ploughmen, tradesmen and their families, had arrived at the thriving Edinburgh metropolis. For most, travelling from the country and from villages with no more than a thousand inhabitants, it must have been a shock to their senses. The grey granite castle dominated the skyline of the Old Town, which had become so overcrowded that many lived alongside the rats in windowless rooms beneath the High Street. However, across a new monumental bridge to Edinburgh New Town lay a more genteel part of the city, occupied by the middle class. Whereas Glasgow had

expanded rapidly, through industry, Edinburgh was home
to banks, insurance companies and stockbrokers, making
it the largest financial centre outside of London. The
population of the city had grown by 50 per cent to 150,000
since the turn of the century, and was further increased
by the transient tourists who were flocking to Scotland,
encouraged by the works of Sir Walter Scott. To cope, eight
mail coaches and fifty stage coaches were leaving the city
every day.[5] Add to this the excitement and apprehension
of the trip ahead and the sadness of leaving families and
friends behind and one can imagine the mental turmoil of
the migrants as they waited in lodgings before being called
to their ship.

At Leith, Edinburgh's port, from where the group was
to depart, things were different, but no better. Dockers
and porters milled around looking for work; sailors sought
their pleasure between voyages and carts clattered along
the cobbled streets, ferrying goods and passengers to the
dockside for onward transfer to their ships. The noise was
relentless, from humans and livestock alike.

One of those ships, the *Symmetry*, was a three-masted
square-rigger, contracted by John Parish Robertson to sail to
Buenos Ayres. She was anchored a couple of miles offshore
on the Leith Roads, an area in the Firth of Forth protected
by the small island of Inverkeith. The waiting passengers
were transported out to the ship by lightermen during the
days prior to departure, and were assigned their cramped
accommodation. Meanwhile, Robertson's agents scurried
around ensuring that final provisions were loaded. On
Sunday, 22 May 1825, the *Symmetry* slipped anchor and
slowly processed out of the Firth of Forth and into open
sea; for the emigrants there was no turning back. However,

within three days those who had spent their lives on the land were suffering another bout of seasickness, and were 'crying out to be set ashore'.[6]

Symmetry

During the next two and a half months, life on board the *Symmetry* was tedious and most of the time William Grierson, in his diary of the voyage, is restricted to a dry account of the weather.[7] The monotony was broken only by the occasional storm, bouts of seasickness and other ailments amongst the passengers, and the birth of children or Grierson's piglets. It was therefore with relief that, at the end of July, land was finally sighted and the *Symmetry* slowly moved from the Atlantic Ocean into the mouth of the River Plate, the widest river in the world. As they passed a point adjacent to Montevideo, the colour of the river gradually changed to a muddy brown, the result of sediment moving down and out of the rivers Parana and Uruguay.

On 8 August the *Symmetry* dropped anchor off Buenos
Ayres. The channels around this port city were difficult and,
as there were no landing piers, moles (sea walls), which
were only accessible at high tide, had to be used. In order
to reach dry land, passengers and equipment had to be
decanted from ship to large rowing boats called whalers,
and from boat to shore by a *carty*. These were extraordinary
horse-drawn carts with large-circumference wheels to
keep both people and goods above water when access to a
mole was not possible. It was a full three days before the
arduous process was complete and all of the prospective
colonists had set foot on the unpaved and muddy roads of
Buenos Ayres. In trepidation, some carried loaded pistols
purchased before they had left Scotland, which, at the very
least, provided some psychological protection against any
perceived threat from the dark-skinned locals speaking in
a strange tongue.

An advance party had already visited the parcel of
land on which they were to settle, but it was not that
which the government had contracted to them. After
signing the contract, the Robertsons had discovered that
the government did not own suitable agricultural land in
the vicinity of Buenos Ayres, so, prior to the arrival of the
Symmetry, they had been forced to purchase a 16,600 acre
plot, in an area called Monte Grande. The land was centred
around the Santa Catalina estate and cost the brothers
around 60,000 pesos (c. £1m), an expenditure that would
return to haunt them.[8]

After a couple of days in Buenos Ayres, the party made
the six-league (c. 36-mile) final leg of their journey using
the traditional method of transport from the city to the
pampas: a train of bullock carts. Six beasts pulled each cart,

which were made entirely of *quebracho* wood, some covered with a *tolda* made from a thatch of small sticks covered with hide in order to protect both passengers and their chattels from the elements. The Scots were apparently unimpressed by Buenos Ayres and so, with relief, the migrants moved out of the city area into the pampas. However, this landscape was also alien to them. The land was flat as far as the eye could see, creating a big sky which, if the weather was fine, was studded with white cotton-wool clouds. Few trees existed to provide depth and colour to the vista and only the hue of the wild verbena and other shrubs broke up the acres of pampas grass swaying in the breeze.

A month, almost to the day, after stepping onto Argentine land, Hugh Robson's wife gave birth to a son, their eighth child, and in recognition of the efforts of the Robertson brothers they named him William Parrish Robson. Hugh's immediate family was now complete, and many years later his great-grandson, John Argentine Campbell, would become the subject of my research as a possible father for Isabel.

The migrants had arrived during the Argentine winter, but, comparing it to Scotland, they must have considered the weather to be mild. In and around Monte Grande, they were likely to have been pleasantly surprised by the habitat and its wildlife. The rivers and lakes harboured lush vegetation where willow and orange trees flourished and parasitic air-plants enjoyed co-existence with the branches of trees. Creepers and reeds grew in abundance and the *cortaderos*, locally known as *cola de zorro* (fox's tail), stood like sentries along the riverbanks. The quacking and flapping of wildfowl would also not have gone unnoticed: there were geese, ducks and storks aplenty. It must have provided a positive first impression, but in the future the migrants would have to endure the negative aspects of the Argentine summer and its, as yet unseen, animals and insects.

The Scottish colonists made a promising start. They were hard-working, God-fearing stock who had risked everything for progress in a new land and were not pre-disposed to let their families down. Within a couple of years the colony had grown and their crops, cheese and butter were being sold in Buenos Ayres. Their success was spelt out in the local English-language press:

> The farmers' houses are generally neat and substantial, of from six to seven apartments each, and the situation of each house is well chosen, commanding a fine, too uninterrupted a prospect over the surrounding pampa; and it would, perhaps, be difficult to find any part in the country so well adapted for the colony as the very estates on which it is happily settled.
>
> The industry and activity which prevail all over the colony are truly praiseworthy, and it cannot but be gratifying to see at this distance from home the members of a little community like this preserving all the sober and moral habits acquired in their own country.
>
> If emigration, organised as this of the Scotch colony has been, were extended in this sphere, who can say to what degree the beneficial effect of such a widened example would have on the agricultural class of this country?[9]

By now, they had witnessed the intolerable heat of the summer, created by the winds from the north, like living with a hairdryer on maximum heat and minimum speed. And when there was some respite, in the form of the cooler southerly winds, it was often preceded by intense thunderstorms and hailstones large enough to kill livestock. They had also encountered spiders the size of one's hand, large iguana, snakes and armadillos, but at least, being so close to Buenos Ayres, they had not come into conflict with the indigenous American Indians.

Many local tribes, descended from the American Indians, populated modern-day Argentina when the Spanish arrived in the sixteenth century. They were not a cohesive group and only offered sporadic or geographically specific resistance to the *conquistadores*, who used them for labour and as slaves. Some tribes resisted the occupation of the land more than others and would attack unprotected ranches. The people of Buenos Ayres province reacted to these attacks by forming the *blandengues* (groups of militia paid for by taxes) in order to drive the indigenous peoples away from their land.[10]

Although the Scottish migrants were not troubled by the indigenous tribes, their successful adaptation was dealt a blow when, in 1827, Rivadavia resigned. The civil war which had been waged on and off since 1814 was now reignited. The new Unitarian leader in Buenos Ayres, General Juan Lavalle, was opposed by the Federalist General Juan Manuel de Rosas, and this augured the beginning of the end for the Monte Grande project. Without Rivadavia, there was no support for the contract that the Robertson brothers had signed, and with the colony sandwiched between the opposing troops life became dangerous and uneconomical. The tradesmen began to move into Buenos Ayres and the women and children started to exit for other parts of the country, leaving the men to manage the land and livestock.

During the next two years, marauding soldiers from both sides attacked properties, within and without the colony, for cash and provisions. In one such incident, the house of the father of Hugh Robson's daughter-in-law, near Canuelas, was attacked and although James Rodger escaped with his life the house was ransacked and burnt to the ground: his pigs were killed and roasted to feed the troops.[11] Hugh Robson's immediate family did not escape this violence either. His son John had been robbed at the family's market stall and when Thomas, John's elder brother, returned they decided to confront the troops to recover cash, which was needed to feed their family. The gang were not impressed and instead turned on John, who was mercilessly shot in the face with a blunderbuss and then 'each with his sword (four of them) stabbed him to death'.[12] So, from a promising start, the Scots were now facing ruin or a risk to their lives.

After the Battle of Puente de Marquez, in April 1829, the civil war ceased and some of the colonists who had moved into the cities for protection gradually returned to their farms. At Monte Grande, they found their properties razed to the ground and livestock stolen or killed. The colony was finished and for the Robertsons it was a financial disaster. For the hard-working colonists, who had already proven that they could succeed on the Argentine pampas, it was a question of dusting themselves down and starting all over in new locations such as Quilmes, San Vicente and Chascomus. The Rodger family, and many others besides those at Monte Grande, also had to start afresh.

Hugh Robson senior remained close to Buenos Ayres and in 1829 became one of the first elders of the newly formed Scotch Presbyterian Chapel, under the pastorship of the Reverend William Brown, formerly of the Monte Grande colony. Such was the religious and social demand from the Scots in and around Buenos Ayres that, in the same year, a subscription plan was put together to raise funds for a new church. In 1830, Thomas Bell was appointed to the Church Committee, the fundraising was a success and in February 1833 the foundation stone was laid for 'the first National Scotch Church in South America'.[13] The new St Andrew's Scotch Presbyterian Church was inaugurated in 1835 and amongst the subscribers that year, for an amount of 200 pesos (c. £3,000), was Hugh Robson, who was to remain an elder of the church until at least 1849.[14] The church, subsequent satellite churches outside of Buenos Ayres and St Andrew's Scots School all became, and are to this day, an essential social focus for Argentine Scots.

By the mid-1830s, almost ten years after his arrival in Argentina, Thomas Bell had become a successful farmer and was playing a full role within the Scottish community. His success and positive reports back home to Innerwick had drawn his brother George and sister Janet to join him. Thomas Bell's other brother, Henry, remained in Dunbar, married Helen Paterson and had four children, but followed, with his family, some time after 1835.

Thomas, who had been the pathfinder, returned to the UK with a view to becoming even more successful. His recently arrived siblings took over the land and the business in Buenos Ayres and Thomas set himself up as a merchant in Liverpool, trading locally, but also exporting much-needed equipment and supplies for George to sell on in Argentina. Thomas remained in Liverpool for the rest of his life.

In 1844 more men from the East Lothian triangle set
sail from Scotland to Buenos Ayres on board the *Prince of
Wales*. The ship was carrying goods bound for George Bell
as well as thirty-six passengers. Amongst them were James
Dodds, born in Cockburnspath; Thomas Drysdale, from
Dunbar and James Burnet, from Whitekirk.[15] All of these
young men from lowland farming stock would have heard
from the Bell family the possibilities awaiting them, and
each would make their own distinct contribution to the
ever-increasing Scottish community in the Argentine.

Shortly after arriving in Argentina, James Dodds took
over the management of George Bell's Magdalena *estancia*,
on the coast seventy miles south of Buenos Ayres. George
and Henry, as well as taking over the management of their
brother Thomas' land, had now built a large portfolio of
farmland and *estancias* on their own account and George
was described by Mulhall as 'one of the chief landed
proprietors in the River Plate'.[16]

Besides Magdalena, there was Viamont, just south
of San Vicente, as well as others in Quilmes, Ensenada
and the province of Banda Oriental. It was on one of
these Bell properties that James Burnet worked before
marrying Henry Bell's second daughter, Elizabeth, in 1847.
The following year his compatriot James Dodds married
Henry's eldest daughter, Isabella, at St Andrew's Church
in Buenos Ayres, and they became brothers-in-law and
life-long friends. James Burnet would later become the
grandfather to John Burnet Campbell, another candidate
in my search for Isabel's father.

In 1851, General de Rosas, who had been in power for
many years, declared war on Brazil. However, the *caudillos*
in Entre Rios, Corrientes and Uruguay, who were not in

favour of de Rosas, signed a treaty with Brazil, creating a new civil uprising. This culminated in the Battle of Caseros, when de Rosas was beaten and deposed by General Justo José de Urquiza. The de Rosas family now faced exile and, as large landowners, began to sell off their properties. James Burnet and James Dodds had been successful enough in the intervening years to take advantage of the situation, and in 1853, together with George Bell, their uncle through marriage, they bought one of the de Rosas' estates.

Estancia La Primera, a thirty-six-square-league estate (c. 275,000 acres), situated in a beautiful area south of Chascomus, was purchased from Don Prudencio de Rosas, the brother of Juan Manuel.[17] Don Prudencio had built the *estancia* house in the 1830s with the rear of the property facing the shore of Laguna del Burro, effectively creating a three-sided property, more easily defendable against attacks from American Indians. To reach the property one had to travel at least ten miles over open countryside before reaching a copse, through which a path was cut. From the cover of the wood a visitor would exit into bright daylight, illuminating the imposing colonnaded porch and crenellated roof of the single-storey *estancia*. The sight remains impressive to this day.

Estancia La Adela, c.1870

Estancia La Juanita, 2014. Formerly Estancia La Adela

The new owners renamed the estate Estancia La Adela and, because of its isolation, they started to develop their own infrastructure. In 1855 Dodds and Burnet opened a school for the children of families working on or near his estate, a practice that remains on large estates in Argentina today. Their next priority was a place of worship, which followed in 1857. The famous Rancho Kirk was a rectangular mud building covered with thatch, situated to the north of the estate near Laguna Yalca, and here, once a month on a Sunday, the Scottish farming community would meet to pray and socialise.

Following years of successful sheep-farming, Burnet and Dodds were, in 1862, able to buy out George Bell's share of the estate. With control solely in their hands, they split the estate; James Burnet's share in the north, closer to Chascomus, was named Estancia San Felipe and Dodds maintained the Adela name and the original house.

By now, the flat pampas countryside south of Buenos Ayres from Santa Catalina through Guardia del Monte, Canuelas, San Vicente and Chascomus was dominated by large tracts of land dedicated to farming sheep for wool and meat. It was here that the Scots excelled and where Mulhall found that 'the neatness, style and good order, both in the estancia house and all its belongings, are very pleasing to the visitor'.[18]

In the 1820s, a number of male inhabitants from the small farming village of Kirkmaiden, on the Whithorn peninsula, in Wigtownshire, Scotland, arrived in Buenos Ayres. They were all successful in their trades or as merchants in Argentina and all were of a similar age. George Campbell, the second son of Alexander and his wife, Margaret Torbron, was born in Kirkmaiden, but had remained in Scotland to farm. All of his children had left the local farming community, except his youngest son Patrick who, as George grew older, remained to help his father on their isolated farm at Balcraig.

When George could no longer cope, he sold up and moved into town to spend his last days at the family home, Prospect House, Newton Stewart,[19] with his deceased wife's sister, Margaret McKie.[20] George's move to Prospect House, in the care of his sister-in-law, released Patrick to lead his own life, and in the knowledge of the earlier migration of his Kirkmaiden neighbours he decided to emigrate to Argentina. Patrick's older brothers had left farming behind years before and had become successful merchants in London and Trinidad, a sign of an educated and ambitious family keen to move away from the harsh life on the exposed peninsula. Patrick was similarly ambitious and was to follow the path of the other Scottish migrant farmers, find success, marry, and father John Burnet Campbell.

On reaching Argentina around 1866, Patrick, the educated son of a landowning farmer with experience of farm management, had no problem in securing work and settled as a shepherd on a farm in Guardia del Monte, 107 miles south of Buenos Ayres. Patrick's great-grand-daughter, in her article, 'On the trail of the Galloway gaucho', suggests that this was a farm owned by James Burnet, and that in providing Patrick with employment he also saw a future suitor for his eldest daughter, Helena.[21] Whether true or not, Patrick would have, in any event, met Helena at one of the monthly Rancho Kirk services.

William McClymont, the son of John, a *Symmetry* immigrant, lived on a neighbouring farm at Monte, and was already making the fifty-mile horse-ride to the Kirk, as did most of the protestant Scots in the area. Patrick would have joined them for this important social gathering, where, in addition to religious solace, news was dispersed and relationships forged. Helena had recently reached a marriageable age and her father would have heard, through the relatives of the Kirkmaiden emigrés, of Patrick's farming abilities and his father's standing in that area. The match was made, either because of a deal with Helena's father or because they fell for each other, and in April 1869, less than three years after Patrick's arrival, they were married at Estancia San Felipe. After the wedding they moved back to Monte, where Patrick continued as a shepherd, and in September that year Helena's brother John and sister Grace, together with James Dodd's son Henry, were also staying with them.[22]

Patrick had some financial security through loans from his father and he received another £500 (c. £32,000) towards the end of 1869.[23] It was the last correspondence with his father, who died a month later. George, in his very detailed will, acknowledged Patrick's sacrifice during the last years of his farming life, by bequeathing him an extra £600 (c. £48,000), in addition to his one-seventh share of the estate. George's will explained that this was because:

> Patrick … has a claim on me for the additional sum herein provided to him, in consideration of the great assistance he rendered to me in the management of my farm during the last three years I was at Balcraig.[24]

With farming success at Monte and the inheritance from his father, Patrick now had the capital to buy his own farm, Estancia San Jorge. It was a significant estate, to the west of Lezama, and the house was approached via a long tree-lined avenue. The farm bordered Laguna de Las Barrancas and was only twenty-five miles south of Helena's parents at San Felipe. Whilst at Monte, Patrick and Helena had two children, George Reid and Elizabeth Ellen, and they were followed by four more, all born at San Jorge: James Burnet in 1875, Alexander Patrick in 1877, John Burnet (Jack) in 1879 and finally William Angus in 1882.

Hugh Robson junior had married the dogged Jane Munroe Rodger in 1840, and Peter, the youngest of Hugh senior's children to have made the *Symmetry* voyage, married Jane Scott, believed to be the daughter of a merchant, at St Andrew's Church, Buenos Ayres, in 1850. As Jane Robson later recalled, in her memoir *Faith Hard Tried*, life was a struggle for many years following her marriage, with tales of attacks by soldiers and local marauders, loss of farm stock due to disease and the premature deaths of two of her sons.[25]

Peter and Jane had moved far away from Buenos Ayres, ending up in Entre Rios, the province north of Buenos Ayres between the River Parana and the River Uruguay, which marks the Uruguayan border. By 1869, Peter and Jane had seven children and his farming enterprise, in the very fertile land near Gualeguay, was obviously a success. Their two elder daughters, Jane and Mary, were at that time residing in Gualeguay itself, receiving private schooling from a Mrs Esperanza Blac;[26] a move which demonstrated the social and economic progress of the Robson family within two generations. It also signalled the birth of a dynasty that would have a lasting influence within Argentina.

In Glasgow, brothers John and Walter Dawson Campbell, the younger sons of John Campbell and Elizabeth Birrell, were also planning to emigrate to Argentina. John was working as an insurance clerk and Walter had recently left school. With little chance of an inheritance, as younger sons, and with a relative already based in Buenos Ayres, the brothers made the decision and by 1871 were in Argentina. Little is known about their first few years in their newly adopted country, yet it did not take them long to make their mark. John became a partner in a textile business, together with Robert Barclay, the son of Robert Barclay and Helen Bond, who were also early colonists from the *Symmetry*.

John was a well-educated, middle-class Scot, whose paternal ancestry can be traced back to the thirteenth century, as a descendant of the Campbells of Strachur, possibly the oldest branch of the Clan Campbell. He was enjoying embryonic commercial success with Barclay & Campbell in Buenos Ayres when he met the refined and very eligible Maria del Rosario Robson, the granddaughter of a Scottish ploughman. The same Mary Robson who, a few years before, was being schooled in Gualeguay and whose successful *estanciero* father was able to provide a suitable dowry. They were married in 1873 and four years later John's brother Walter Dawson married Mary's younger sister Margaret.

By 1875, fifty years after the arrival of the *Symmetry*, the extended family living in Argentina related to Hugh Robson senior, the poor ploughman from Dumfriesshire, totalled in excess of 120, and were on the whole successful landowners, merchants and brokers. The farming stock from Torthorwald, the East Lothian triangle and Kirkmaiden had settled and become ranchers, and the Campbells from Edinburgh had become successful *comerciantes*. Many prayed, worked and celebrated together, and married within this tight-knit Scottish migrant group. Their lives had not been easy, but the fruits of their labour and their determination and courage were now shining through.

2

From the Land to the Landed

Success is to be measured not so much by the position that one has reached in life as by the obstacles which he has overcome.

Booker T. Washington

I n 1865 life changed dramatically for those who had settled between Chascomus and Buenos Ayres, when the first Argentine railroad was opened between those two communities. Farmers were able to transport livestock more quickly and absentee *estancia* owners were able to move more regularly between their city homes and the camp, as the pampas countryside was called. As the railroad across Argentina developed, land values rocketed and the already wealthy farmers became even wealthier.

Outside of the rail network, to the south-west of Buenos Ayres, Inés Faria Mujica owned 18,500 acres of land, which she had never visited. She also owed a substantial amount to Barclay & Campbell, for purchases she had made from their textile business, and in 1875 offered the land to satisfy the debt. The partners accepted the offer and two years later Robert Barclay, who was not interested in the land and probably needed the cash, was bought out by John Campbell. The estate was located between Carlos Casares and Quiroga, over 200 miles from Buenos Ayres, and John immediately bought additional contiguous parcels of land creating a total estate of 45,000 acres, which he called Estancia La Corona.[1]

The estate was in a remote part of Buenos Ayres province still inhabited by American Indians, though these tribes were less aggressive than those in the northern area of the pampas, who still fought to defend their land. It would be another four years before General Julio A. Roca led his army to purge the pampas of the indigenous population once and for all. The driving out of the indigenous people from their settlements was considered necessary in order that more land could be farmed in safety. The attacks were financed by the sale of large tracts of government land and became known as the 'Conquest of the Desert', but more recently have been recognised as an act of genocide.

With John managing his affairs in Buenos Ayres he sent his younger brother Walter Dawson Campbell, known as Strachur, to secure and guard the land at Carlos Casares. Not that he could have achieved much, other than flee on horseback at the first whiff of an Indian incursion. Strachur and his men slept with their ears to the ground listening out for any approaching Indian *malon*. Their horses would remain saddled during the night for a swift getaway, and when the warning was given they would ride off to the protection of the fort at Nueve de Julio. However, more often than not these were false alarms created by the sound of the burrowing native tuco-tuco rodents. The estate avoided attack during this time, and Strachur's tenure was a success as a mud building, similar in size and style to the Rancho Kirk, was erected and remains intact today in the grounds of La Corona.

Original building at Estancia La Corona

By 1877 John Campbell owned the large estate at Carlos Casares, a business in Buenos Ayres, and a villa at Devoto in the *partido* of Flores, which at that time was in the countryside outside of the city. It was here, on 31 October, that John Argentine Campbell was born. The birth of his first son and heir was auspicious for John senior, who christened him in his own name and that of his father, but also added the name of his adopted country. Despite John's combination of Robson and Campbell genes, of brain and brawn, of piety and affluence, none could have foreseen the mark that the life of this man would leave upon the world.

John Argentine grew up in the relatively peaceful environment of Flores, away from the noise, dirt and hurly-burly of the fast-growing port-city of Buenos Ayres. It is possible that he never visited Estancia La Corona during his formative years as, without a railway connection, the journey would have taken days by bullock cart or on horseback. More likely he remained at home, was tutored and later attended St Andrew's Scots School in the city, nine miles away.

John Campbell senior

John senior had long held a desire to make his fortune and buy back the estate and lairdship of the Campbells of Strachur, which had been held by his ancestors.[2] They had bypassed his family because, generations before, a complex entailment allowed the estate to pass to a female Campbell instead of maintaining the rule of male primogeniture. With this in mind, John considered the long-term future of his son, with schooling a priority.

Fettes College had opened in Edinburgh in 1870, supported by an endowment from Sir William Fettes. Fettes made his fortune trading in tea during the Napoleonic war, and in memory of his only child, William, who had died of typhoid, he wanted to provide education for orphaned or needy children. The trustees of the endowment took their time to find land and build the school, which did not open until thirty-four years after Sir William's death. It immediately took fee-paying as well as foundation scholars and quickly gained a positive reputation. Even the liberal Walter Wren, the famous tutor who ran a crammer for potential entrants to a military college and the Indian Civil Service, commented 'the education there seems to be perhaps the best that I know of'.[3]

Sending John to a Scottish boarding school, which was run along the lines of an English public school, would not only provide him with everlasting Scottish roots, but could also provide culture and status appropriate for a potential (in John senior's eyes) clan chief. And so, in the summer of 1887, in a state of nervous apprehension, John and his parents sailed from Buenos Ayres for Edinburgh. He was leaving the home of his birth for the land of his birthright, to be educated as a Scottish gentleman. After a ten-week sea voyage and an overland journey to Edinburgh, John must have been awestruck upon glimpsing the college for the first time: a gothic edifice in the sombre grey of Edinburgh stone.

Leaving a child at an educational establishment may have been the norm for the gentry in nineteenth-century Britain, but its outcome, positive or negative, could not be known until some years had passed. In John's case, one may now assume with hindsight that it was positive, but on that day in 1887, as John may have bravely fought back the tears, who could have known. He had not even turned ten, and was big-boned and rounded with puppy fat, creating cannon-fodder for even the mildest of tormentors that awaited him. His parents bade John farewell and good wishes, neither knowing the next time they would see each other, nor indeed when John would return to the Argentine.

Fettes College was renowned for its academic and sporting achievements, but also for its spartan environment. For John, school life began at Kimmerghame House, the junior boarding dormitory of the college, where his contemporaries recall their initial impressions of dampness, the pervading smell of carbolic soap and varnish, and the minute cubicles that awaited them. Each cubicle contained a small bed, under which was placed a tin bath filled with water, a couple of drawers and a washstand. The dormitory windows remained open in all but the fiercest of weather, and it was not unusual for the scholars to have to break the ice in their baths with a hairbrush before they could wash. The harsh daily routine became as habitual as the monotony of the food, which consisted mainly of porridge and bread.[4]

John would have spent exeats and holidays with family and friends in the UK, as time would never permit him to make the journey back to Argentina, although he did enjoy a couple of summers with his parents, who journeyed to the UK in 1892 and 1895. Over time, puppy fat disappeared, pubescence passed and John became a strapping young man, excelling in all forms of sport. The 'Fatty Campbell' epithet that had greeted him in 1887 was now history and he had become revered throughout the school.[5] His life and stature towards the end of his time at Fettes is best summarised by his contemporary J. A. Stevenson, an author and journalist who became the *Times* correspondent in Canada:

the great hero of the school, John Campbell of
Moredun, [John's senior boarding house] one of
the race of Argentine Scots who have persistently
maintained their tie with the land of their forebears
sending their sons home to it for their education.
Endeared with a magnificent physique, had been
in both cricket and football teams for aeons and
ended his career as captain of both with the dual
school championship to his credit. He was a born
leader of men and boys and his word was literally
law throughout the school, but withal he was a
singularly modest boy upon whom his laurels
sat lightly and he well deserved the aura of fame
which clung to his name years after his departure. [6]

In the summer of 1897, John went up to Trinity
College, Cambridge, and in his freshman year was awarded
his rugby 'Blue' by Osbert Gadesden Mackie, the captain of
Cambridge who, in the previous year as an undergraduate,
was chosen to tour with the British Lions to South Africa.
John played in the varsity matches in 1897, 1898 and
1899, captaining the formidable Cambridge team in the
latter year, when all of the forwards, including John, gained
international honours. [7] John played for Scotland against
Ireland on 24 February 1900, a scoreless draw, but was
unable to turn out for the match against England later that
year as he had returned to Argentina.

John had been away for thirteen years and would hardly
have recognised the city of Buenos Ayres. Not only had it
spread to the countryside of his birthplace, but motor cars now
competed with the horse-drawn trams and carriages for space
on the narrow streets. John could also more easily visit the
estancia at Carlos Casares, which now had a railway station
following the extension from Chivilqoy to St Rosas in 1890.

Here, on the La Corona estate, close to the original mud hut, John senior had built a magnificent estancia house. It was a rectangular white building with an elegant porticoed entrance, and windows with iron grilles, a remnant of the need to protect against attack. Inside were fittings and furniture imported from Europe, a statement of success in the Argentine.

John Argentine (left) and Roderick Campbell

However, John's return to Argentina was short-lived as, in October, he travelled back to the UK with his brother, Roderick, to take up a position as Assistant Master at Loretto School in Edinburgh.

Patrick, the father of John Burnet Campbell (Jack), had built a successful farming enterprise following his purchase of Estancia San Jorge in 1873. He had remained in the pampas as his children grew up, but in 1890, with the education of his younger sons in mind, he decided to move to the city. George Reid, his eldest son, had, as his uncles from Balcraig, already decided not to pursue a life on the ranch, instead opting for a commercial career. Also the railroad had been extended from Chascomus and a station built at Lezama, allowing Patrick to make regular visits from Buenos Ayres to keep an eye on his farm.

He found an imposing townhouse at the southern end of the *barrio* of San Telmo, an area in the city preferred by the upper classes at the turn of the century. It was probably a two-storey, well-proportioned and imposing property similar to others which can still be seen on Avenida Caseros. It would have been large enough for the whole family and was conveniently situated within a few blocks of Estacion Constitucion, the terminus for the train to Chascomus and Lezama.

Jack was sent to the newly opened Lomas Academy, in Lomas de Zamora, a few miles south of their Buenos Ayres home and accessible on the same train line to Chascomus. The school was conceived in 1890 by local English-speaking residents who wanted an educational establishment in the style of an English public school, and it still operates today, as Barker College. Here, Jack excelled at cricket, as did his brothers, Alexander and William.

A year later, the neighbouring Lomas Academy Athletic Club was founded by, amongst others, Thomas Dodds, a land surveyor and the son of James of Estancia La Adela. The club, two years later, changed its name to the Lomas Athletic Club and is one of the oldest clubs still in existence in Argentina, and a pivotal organisation in terms of sport. Lomas Athletic was considered one of the first great football teams of Argentina; in 1899 it was one of the four founding clubs of the River Plate Rugby Championship, the forerunner of the Argentine Rugby Union, and in 1912 it hosted one of the three first-class cricket matches between Argentina and the MCC. The first of these cricket matches was played at the Hurlingham Club, and the Argentine team included John Argentine, another testament to his sporting prowess.

The lives of the Scottish migrant families, by this time, with their private schools and clubs, and their estates and city homes, was far removed from the Scotland their ancestors had left behind. But, rather than laud the efforts and sacrifices of their forebears, it seems that the successful descendants of the migrants no longer wished to be associated with their peasant ancestry. Their origins had been clearly laid out in articles written by James Dodds, but when these were published in book form, as *Records of the Scottish Settlers in the River Plate*, in 1897, many were bought up and destroyed. Very few original copies exist today. [8]

Once Jack had completed his schooling, he continued his cricket, playing a season for the Belgrano second eleven. He then joined the Lomas Athletic Club second team on probation, before being promoted to the Lomas first team in 1899. He continued to play for Lomas for over twenty more years, where he was considered a first-rate bat, and captained the first team in at least seven of those seasons. [9] Meanwhile, his father, who had taken to drink, was slipping into a state of alcoholic dementia. [10]

Although Patrick had remained close to his farming pedigree, Jack and his brothers were destined for commerce. Jack first joined Juan y Jose Drysdale y Cia, a merchant company specialising in agricultural equipment.

The company was founded by relatives of Thomas Drysdale, who had travelled from East Lothian on the *Prince of Wales*, and who had been born in a neighbouring village to Jack's grandfather, James Burnet.

Jack's mother died in 1907 and around this time he moved to another merchant, Ashworth y Cia, but continued living with his father and brothers. Finally, in 1912, Jack set up his own merchanting partnership, Campbell & Carlisle.

John Burnet Campbell c. 1918

By 1904, John Argentine had settled permanently back in Argentina and his father's La Corona estate was split. John was given 20,000 acres, which he named Estancia El Jabali; 5,000 acres were destined for Roderick, and the remainder of La Corona stayed with John Campbell senior, on the understanding that it would eventually pass to his daughter, Leila. Over ten years earlier, John's family had been instrumental in helping to set up the Hurlingham Club on the outskirts of Buenos Ayres. John's father and paternal uncle provided financial support and his maternal uncle, Hugh Scott Robson, provided both finance and a plot of land adjacent to a new railroad, running north out of Buenos Ayres. In 1888 John senior was present at the meeting which drew up the legal statutes of the club, modelled on the Hurlingham in England, which would over the years provide both sporting and social facilities, including cricket, rugby, soccer, horse-racing and, most importantly, polo. The mastermind behind the development of the club was William Lacey, who had been the cricket professional at Oundle School, before moving to Canada to coach and play. He was only twenty-eight when appointed manager/coach of the club and his legendary son, Lewis, became the first ten-handicap polo player in Argentina and a close friend of John.

Besides working on his *estancia*, it was polo which took up most of John's time and also that of his brother, Roderick. Polo had been an integral part of *estancia* life at La Corona, which had its own polo field close to the imposing residence that John senior had built. It was in this environment of breeding and training polo ponies and playing polo that John met his future wife, Myra Gertrude Grant; by all accounts, an indomitable horse tamer. Little is known of the courtship of John and Myra and how romantically linked they may have been, but in later life circumstances indicate that there may have been a coolness or emotional detachment to Myra's character.

Estancia La Corona, 2014

In 1904 tragedy hit the Campbell family with the untimely death of Roderick, in an unlucky sequence of events. At the beginning of March, Roderick slipped on some rotten fruit on a pavement; a banana skin moment that was to go horribly wrong. Roderick's left forearm had been broken, yet four days later, presumably with his arm strapped, he made the mistake of playing polo again.[11] He fell badly and smashed his collarbone.[12] This time, there was to be no quick recovery as, at the beginning of April, he was still an in-patient at the British Hospital in Buenos Ayres. No doubt restless at being incarcerated in the hospital, Roderick took some time out of his bed, caught a chill, inflamed his lungs and died.[13] A year later, John married Myra and on 29 May 1906 they had their first child, a son who they named Roderick, and who years later would also die in unusual circumstances.

Within a couple of years John was one of only four nine-handicap polo players in Argentina; the others were the legendary Lewis Lacey, John's uncle Hugh Scott Robson and Joseph Traill.[14] The Robson family was considered the leading polo family of Argentina, with three of Hugh's brothers also excellent players. Hugh, however, was the best, winning six Open Championships in Argentina and described as 'an ambidextrous player in an epoch during which it was legal to hit the ball with either hand, and a superb horseman to boot'.[15]

This was the environment in which John lived his life. He was a gifted sportsman who was awarded Blues at Cambridge for rugby, athletics and cricket, and almost made the rowing eight. Now he was leading his own Western Camps polo team, with whom he won two Open Championships, in 1907 and 1909.[16] John was egalitarian and a meritocrat when it came to choosing his team, as it included *peons* (farmworkers) who had natural horse-riding skills. Such was his success that when the Western Camps won the Open for the second time, in 1909, the Polo Association of the River Plate prohibited *peons* in all official tournaments.[17] What appeared to be a case of sour grapes or even snobbery (they continued to allow *estancia* administrators and managers) was not reversed until 1920, after the end of a war which would take so many of Argentina's migrant population.

John and Myra had a second son, John Douglas (Tony), on 29 April 1907 and in 1912, in what was probably the climax of John's polo career, he visited England as a member of Harold Schwind's El Bagual team. Schwind financed the trip to compete in the 1912 polo season at the English Hurlingham Club. El Bagual reached the final of the Social Clubs' Cup, where they outplayed the Bath Club to win comfortably. Later they also won the Whitney Cup, with

John replacing an injured teammate in the final. John stepped admirably up to the plate, making 'two of the best runs, which ended successfully in this game, that were seen during the season'.[18] English polo circles were in shock and rather patronisingly described the Argentine ponies as holding their own well against the best of the British ones. Argentine polo had made its very indelible mark, both for the quality of its ponies and the skill of its players, only one of whom, John, was born in Argentina.

The Hurlingham experience must have had a positive impact on John, who returned to the UK in February 1913 on the *Arlanza*. He travelled with Myra, but without the children, and although the trip was probably a mix of business, possibly involving the sale of polo ponies, and pleasure, he did manage to join a scratch polo team called the Rovers. His cousin, Hugh Noel Scott Robson, played against him but John competed successfully and his team won the Ranelagh Novices' Cup in June.[19] It would be the last time he played polo in the UK: he returned to Argentina to continue managing his and his ailing father's *estancias*.

By 1914, as the cloud of conflict began to engulf Europe, the Scots in Argentina continued to flourish and contribute to the community, building churches, opening clubs and schools, and enhancing the emerging Argentine Republic by their presence. Rugby, soccer, tennis, cricket, polo and horse-racing were developed and enjoyed, albeit initially by the middle class, after being introduced by the migrant families. The Scots were only a small portion of the total immigration pool which settled in Argentina in the nineteenth century, with the English, Welsh, Germans, Italians and Spanish all contributing to the cosmopolitan tapestry of the country.

However, the small cadre of families from a few Scottish lowland locations had made a relatively bigger impact. The Robsons, Bells, Campbells, Burnets and Dodds, amongst others, all played a major role in the development of the young Argentine state and are weaved through the ancestry of John Argentine and John Burnet Campbell.

3

The Making of Jock

It is indeed a desirable thing to be well-descended,
but the glory belongs to our ancestors.

Plutarch

I n 1880, far removed from the pampas and to parents even further removed from the lowland Scottish migrant farmers, Otto Campbell Philippi was born. As his name suggests, he had through his mother, Mary Campbell Gibson, a link to Scotland, and coincidentally to Leith, where his great-grandfather had, in 1797, founded a shipping company, and from where the *Symmetry* had sailed fifty-five years previously. Despite the maternal link to Scotland, his mother was born and lived her life in Hamburg and in 1879 had married Otto Heinrich Philippi, a wealthy and successful businessman. More than twenty years would pass before Otto Campbell Philippi became known as John Otto Campbell (Jock), and many more before research would identify him as the third potential father for Isabel.

Jock was a fifth-generation direct descendant of

Alexander David, a Court Jew and agent and Imperial Factor to successive dukes of Brunswick. Alexander was born in Halberstadt, Prussia, in January 1687, and in 1707, as a penniless twenty-year-old, he moved to Brunswick to eke out a living. His prospects were not good as Jews had been expelled from the city in the 1550s and his arrival would not have been readily accepted. Nevertheless, he seems to have been intelligent, resourceful and streetwise, quickly building a reputation for being able to source goods not found locally and giving a personal service that other traders were unable, or did not wish, to provide. Within a few years Alexander was able to count Augustus, the heir to the Dukedom of Brunswick, as one of his supporters and, in return for services rendered, Augustus promised him many favours if, and when, he became Duke.[1]

Alexander David in 1760

Upon the succession of Augustus, in 1714, Alexander became unbelievably prominent within the court, initially being granted permission to build a house, set up a tobacco factory and import luxury goods.[2] Complaints were made by the gentile courtiers to the duke, who is said to have responded, 'will one ever find his equal, blessed with such divine inventive genius'.[3] Over the ensuing fifty years, Alexander became indispensable to the court and in return amassed a fortune. As a devout Jew, in an otherwise mostly non-Jewish city, Alexander, in his spare time, studied the Talmud, collected Jewish antiquities and built a synagogue within his home. By the time he died, at the age of eighty, more than thirty-three Jewish families had become established in Brunswick and his collection was so valuable and religiously significant that he left it to the state. Today, the artefacts form a small part of the Jewish Museum of Brunswick, with much more remaining in storage or on loan to other museums. Alexander's rise, from rags to riches, from unacceptable to influential Jew, provided a dynastic legacy, with his descendants becoming famous theologians, entrepreneurs, bankers, pioneers and industrialists.

Alexander's grandson, Ludwig Alexander David was born in 1770 in Altona, a small town outside of Hamburg. In the years that followed, at the end of the eighteenth century, Jewish emancipation spread through Austria and Prussia and, in return for granting equality to Jews, the government made it a condition that Jews must adopt a Germanic surname. In 1786 Ludwig changed his surname to Philipson (son of Philip, his father), in line with Jewish tradition at that time. This period of emancipation also coincided with an increase in the number of converts from Judaism to Christianity, mainly by the educated middle-class, who had the most to benefit from the increased opportunities of being a Christian. In 1813 Ludwig and his family converted to Lutheranism and in a final break with their Jewish roots officially changed their surname to Philippi in 1818.[4]

Ludwig's children included Martin, a theologian who became rector at Solingen, and Hermann, John Otto Campbell's (Jock's) grandfather, who was a partner in the family banking business, J. Magnus & Co. The families of these two brothers were very close: one of Martin's sons began work at Hermann's bank and another, Ernst, married Hermann's daughter, Magda.

Hermann Philippi

Hermann married Elise Krüger in 1847, but her health did not hold and, after bearing three children, including Jock's father, Otto Heinrich (Otto), she died in 1856. The following year Hermann married his first wife's cousin Marie Schindeler, who bore him four more children.

Together, despite the political unrest in Germany at that time, they enjoyed a fabulous lifestyle: idyllic summers at their country house at Lokstedt, and the rest of the year in their palatial city home on Hermannstrasse in Hamburg.

Hermann's nephew Ernst, who would play a key role in Jock's life, had, unlike his theologian father, inherited the family entrepreneurial genes. He had started work in his uncle's bank but found the environment stifling and the menial tasks repetitive. Instead, Ernst spread his wings and in 1866 moved to Manchester, England, to become a cotton trader, in a business run by another uncle, Eduard. After a short time he set himself up as a trader in his own right, and following some successful small trades he expanded overseas and started to enter into speculative trading. In 1872, after the necessary qualifying years of residence in the UK, Ernst applied and was accepted as a naturalised British citizen. He then proposed to his cousin Magda, who, following their wedding in May 1873, joined Ernst in Liverpool.

Otto Ernst Philippi

Unfortunately, the exuberance and confidence of youth led Ernst to over-extend the business and his financial position became very precarious. He was forced to sell a horse harness and gig in April 1875,[5] and between May and August he was teeming and lading with client's money and stock. In the autumn Ernst was prosecuted and his parents had to bail him out of prison to avoid the ignominy of him being remanded in custody. The Philippi archives suggest that the intervention was to keep Ernst out of debtor prison, which would have brought shame on the family in Germany.

Mr Justice Mellor heard the case at Liverpool Crown Court on 12 December, but it did not last long. Ernst's attorney made a lengthy legal argument that he had not committed the offences, and the judge, also believing that the prosecution had failed to make their case, had no option but to acquit him. It was a hollow victory for Ernst, as the judge commented that his actions were very improper if not illegal.[6] It's also possible that Ernst's parents paid off all of his debts, thus satisfying any potential negative witnesses. But his family also extracted their price: they only provided the financial support after Ernst had promised to forsake all speculative ideas and return to work, in Germany, in a commercial position, however modest.

Having agreed, Ernst moved back and joined Nicolai Wulff, an agent for the UK J. & P. Coats company, importing cotton thread into Germany. He was employed to handwrite correspondence in English to Coats HQ in Paisley, Scotland, and to avoid the tedium he ensured that each of the letters was perfect in form and content, before submitting to his manager for signature. He was true to his promise and remained deskbound at Wulff until, in 1878, Archibald Coats, the head of the Coats business, made a surprise visit to his agent's office in Hamburg. Holding a letter in his hand, Archibald asked to speak to the person who wrote it. Ernst's manager said that it was his letter, but Archibald demanded to meet the writer not the signatory. The manager admitted that it was Ernst who had been writing the letters and effectively negotiating with J. & P. Coats for a number of years.

Archibald was escorted to the back office and introduced to Ernst; a very short interview followed.

'Did you write this letter?' asked Coats.

'Yes,' replied Ernst.

'Then I engage you to join my company. You must come immediately, to Paisley, to familiarise yourself, then I have a task for you in Greece.'[7]

A few days later Ernst was in Paisley. He successfully completed the project in Greece, after which he was asked to go to Argentina, and by the end of 1878 he was Foreign Sales Manager earning £500 (c. £ 45,000) per annum.[8]

Ernst's cousin Otto had also broken with tradition and, influenced by playing within the farming community of Lokstedt during his childhood summers, he enrolled at the Grand Duchy of Saxony Agricultural College in Jena. This adventure into farming was short-lived and he moved on to the University of Göttingen to study under Professor Friedrich Wöhler, the pioneer of organic chemistry. His studies were abruptly halted when war broke out against France in July 1870, and soon after he was fighting in northern France as part of the 7th Uhlan (lancers) Regiment. Otto had an honourable campaign fighting in battles around Amiens and then returned to Göttingen to complete his doctorate.

Otto Heinrich Philippi

As a bright young chemist in his early twenties, Otto had no problem in finding significant positions in the chemical factories of Hamburg, and by 1876 he was ready to embark upon his own enterprise. He teamed up with Dr Carl Beit, another chemist and son of the founder of the German chemical industry, Ferdinand Beit. Together they formed a company, Beit & Philippi, and set up a factory on a five acre site on Dorotheenstrasse, producing, amongst other things, potash salts, camphor and printing inks. They were particularly successful in the latter, becoming the world's largest supplier of quality lithographic ink by the turn of the century.[9]

Three years passed as Otto grew his business, then, in 1879 at the age of thirty, he married Mary Campbell Gibson, the daughter of William Gibson, a shipbroker who had died some years earlier. William, the son of George Gibson of Leith, had moved to Hamburg with his wife, Isabella, and his brother Alexander, and set up a shipbroking business, linked to their father's company, George Gibson & Co. After William's death, Isabella remained in Hamburg with her children, Mary, Adela, Edina and William, and married Mr R. J. Pearson, another shipbroker, who had offices in the same street as her first husband.

Mary Campbell Philippi (née Gibson)

On 6 July 1880, in Hamburg, Mary Campbell Philippi gave birth to her first son, Otto Campbell Philippi (Jock). Jock's family was rich in history and highly successful but, although much was expected of him, his path in life was not to be an easy one.

In 1883 Richard Philippi was born, providing a brother for Jock and completing Otto and Mary's family. The two boys were exposed to the English language from birth, through their mother, at school, and from other family members, some of whom were working in the UK. Family life in Hamburg would have been extremely comfortable as not only were the Philippis successful and well connected in their own right, they were associated, through Mary, to successful shipping businesses and through Otto to the extended Beit family, which was considered to have wealth in excess of that of the Rockefellers or the Rothschilds.

During the 1880s Hamburg became the leading emigration port from the continent of Europe and witnessed the final mass emigration of Germans to America, many of whom were Roman Catholics escaping the anti-Catholic *kulturkampf* of Otto von Bismarck. Things became bleak in Hamburg in 1892, when they suffered the last major outbreak of cholera to have occurred in a major city, claiming 8,500 lives. It was also a bad year for Beit & Philippi: on 21 December a fire completely gutted the central block of their factory, where saltpetre was manufactured.[10] However, the Philippis survived both and the factory was quickly rebuilt.

Two years later the family was rocked by the sudden death of Otto, at the young age of forty-five. Left behind were Jock, fourteen; Richard, twelve; and Mary, a thirty-six-year-old widow. Ten years previously, following the rapid growth of the Beit & Philippi company, Carl's brother Gustav Beit had joined the company as a third partner, and after the death of Otto the two Beit brothers bought out Otto's share from his widow and changed the name of the business to Beit & Co.

Either through Otto's will or the intestacy laws of Germany at that time, Jock and Richard would have inherited a share of their father's estate, which would have been held in trust until they attained the age of twenty-one.

One can only imagine the turmoil faced by this young family following the early death of their father and husband, but life continued and Mary was soon to find another partner, Francisco Xavier de Gisbert (Francis).

Jock grew up in one of Europe's largest port cities and his maternal family had shipping in their blood. His mother's father and stepfather were both shipbrokers in Hamburg and George, her grandfather, had founded a shipping business in Scotland, a company that remains in operation to this day. With his brother, Richard, at school in Oldenburg, his mother in a burgeoning relationship with Francis and the sudden loss of his father still raw, Jock ran away, reaching Cardiff, Wales, in June 1897. It is not surprising that the shipping connections led him towards a life at sea, though his sudden disappearance shocked the family.

At Cardiff on 4 June, he blagged his way onto the coasting vessel *Maria* out of Gloucester and, although only sixteen, inflated his age to eighteen and fabricated prior experience on the *Callispa*.[11] The *Maria* sailed out of Cardiff on 9 June and made its way to Kinsale in Ireland. Its crew list, registered at Kinsale on 30 June, described 'James Otto Campbell Philippi' as an able seaman, but by the time the *Maria* returned to its home port of Gloucester, around 17 August, the truth was out. Jock had been downgraded from able seaman to 'boy' and was discharged.[12] However, this early ability to manufacture an escape to another country and create a fiction around him presaged a romantic and adventurous future.

Possibly traced by his concerned family, Jock then travelled, or was taken, to Scotland, where he lived for the next twelve months at Warren Park, Largs, with his Aunt Magda and Uncle Ernst. His youthful adventure at sea had been cut short. Ernst had now been working for J. & P. Coats for almost twenty years and had become phenomenally successful. He had travelled extensively, set up many overseas subsidiaries and in the process had negotiated a percentage, for himself, on newly generated business. It was a prime example of the Philippi entrepreneurial gene, which had almost been contained in 1875, when his family forced him to return to Germany. Now it had made him an extremely wealthy and relatively famous British businessman.

A few months later, in January 1898, in London, Mary Campbell Philippi married the charismatic Francis, an engineer based in Hamburg. Jock may have been somewhat surprised that his mother was marrying someone ten years younger, but Francis was an extraordinary character, who not only made his mother happy, but also had the ability to win Jock's approval. Francis was the son of his namesake, Francisco J. de Gisbert, who was born in Murcia and had been the Spanish Consul in Newcastle before transferring to Germany. Francis spoke many languages, was a musician, a sportsman and was developing a passion for adventure. After their wedding, Mary and Francis returned to Hamburg, where they lived in an apartment on Hartwicusstrasse, overlooking the Mundsburger Kanal.

During his year at Warren House, Jock spent most of his time with his cousin Alexander being tutored, but also relaxing, playing and planning his future. Ernst saw in Jock the same headstrong streak that had caused himself so much trouble thirty years previously, but knew that, if nurtured, Jock could make a success of his life. Ernst was a man of great intellect, a linguist, highly successful and now a father figure for Jock. During the year, Jock grew closer to Ernst and listened intently to tales of Ernst's travels and in particular those about Argentina, a land of great promise. Jock, now eighteen, was not cut out for university, would not inherit for several years and needed more time to develop. Whether via Ernst; his new stepfather, Francis; or another member of his family with shipping connections, Jock became aware of the Brassey Scheme, which aimed to 'provide a professional education for the sons of gentlemen whilst training them to become officers in the Mercantile Marine'.[13]

The scheme, launched in 1890, was named after Lord Brassey, a politician who became Lord of the Admiralty, and was developed in conjunction with the shipping company Devitt & Moore. Although a niche operation, it was one that was much needed as there was a shortage of merchant naval officers to take up positions in the ever-expanding steamship business. There was no ocean-based, i.e. on-the-job, officer training available and the sea apprentice system had become abused: on many ships the apprentices were used as cheap labour and learnt nothing that would prepare them for the higher ranks. By comparison, the Brassey Scheme provided training in seamanship as well as a practical education. As midshipmen, the members of this scheme were provided with well-equipped cabins, a large mess room and were looked after by stewards. However, it was far from an easy life.

The Brassey Scheme clippers sailed between London and Australia and at the end of the nineteenth century these full-sail ships were in competition with steam. It was up to the trainee officers to ensure that voyage times were kept to a minimum, and all were required to master the handling of sail, high above the deck, in all weathers. This required mental and physical stamina and teamwork.

At other times during the ninety-day voyage the young men had to cope with the monotony of the routine at sea.

Devitt & Moore's Australian sailing ships *Macquarie* and *Hesperus* had been specially adapted so that up to thirty trainee officers could be accommodated. In addition to the standard complement of officers the training ships carried a naval instructor, who taught seamanship during a four-hour watch and provided lessons in arithmetic, algebra, trigonometry, navigation and nautical astronomy when the midshipmen were not on watch. Unlike apprentices, who also worked alongside the midshipmen, they did not sign indentures. Instead, they signed the ship's articles for one voyage at a time, but the total premium for the, up to five, voyages needed to obtain the necessary sea time to apply for a Certificate of Competency as a Second Mate could cost as much as £300 (c. £30,000). By comparison a four-year apprenticeship cost £30.[14] The additional cost was explained by the Brassey midshipmen having stewards to attend them, whereas apprentices looked after themselves.

In October 1898 Jock entered the scheme, financed by his mother and stepfather, and gave his contact address as that of F. J. de Gisbert in Hamburg.[15] On 16 October 1898 Jock was on board the *Hesperus*, being towed out of the East India Dock, London, en route to Melbourne, Australia.[16] One can imagine Jock's nervous excitement as he embarked on this adventure in the company of fellow trainees, some much younger, and almost all the sons of the English middle class.

The Master of the *Hesperus* was Captain Charles Maitland, a man eminently qualified 'for the arduous task of controlling and teaching a shipload of thirty or forty high-spirited boys'.[17] The clipper reached Melbourne on

4 January 1899 and set out for its return to London on 18 February.[18] After eight months at sea Jock arrived back in London and made his way to Harrogate, where he stayed with his Aunt Adela and her husband, James Culross, a printing manager.

The Culross brothers, James and Allan, were linked, in some way, to Jock's father's printing ink business during the 1880s. Neither feature in the UK Census of 1881 and it is possible that they were working for Beit & Philippi in Hamburg. Both married sisters of Jock's mother in Hamburg, but by 1891 had returned with their wives to the UK. Allan set up his own business as a printing ink maker in London and by 1911 James was a Master Printer in Harrogate.

Jock returned to London six weeks later to join the *Macquarie*, the most famous of the Devitt & Moore training ships. Built in 1875 and initially named the *Melbourne*, it was unusual: a frigate-styled clipper built of iron. It was also very large for a sailing ship, registered at 1,852 tons and with a length of 269 feet, and one of only three of its style ever built. The *Melbourne* had been sailing between London and Victoria, Australia, until 1887, when Devitt & Moore acquired her, changed her name to *Macquarie* and her route to Sydney. Jock must have been impressed with the magnificence of the ship, with her long line of painted portholes and gilded imitation windows at the stern, reminiscent of the frigates of a bygone age. Inside, her cedar-panelled cabins gleamed and a special schoolroom for the midshipmen had been constructed between decks.

On board Jock met fellow trainee Hugh Geoffrey Coker Adams, who was making his second voyage to Sydney.[19] On his first trip, in 1898, Hugh Adams had kept a detailed log, which gives an insight into the life that Jock would have experienced at sea.[20] On board were around forty midshipmen, seventeen apprentices, four officers and fourteen crew. Typically, each Sunday, a service was held on the poop deck, with the help of the ship's band. At other times during the voyage sports and games were arranged on deck, including cricket, tennis and hockey. Within twenty days out of London Adams recalls sighting whales, flying fish and sea snakes in the southern Atlantic. Forty days out, albatross, porpoise and more whales, and several days later he notes that the watch was on the lookout for ice. In between the relatively few social activities on an eighty-day voyage, the midshipmens' time was filled with deck washing, lifeboat drill, furling and unfurling of sails in all weathers, and painting and cleaning the ship. For Hugh's return journey the *Macquarie* took on board a cargo of wool, timber, tallow, meat and hides. He also notes the illnesses that occurred in the midshipmen and apprentices: sometimes seasickness but also 'fever and ague'.[21] Such was Jock's new life at sea.

On returning from Sydney, Jock was able to take over two month's break, again with the Culross family at Tower House, in Harrogate. In July 1900 he returned to London for his third and final voyage, again on the *Macquarie* and again in the company of Hugh Adams. Whilst Jock was away his grandfather Hermann had passed away in Hamburg at the age of eighty-seven. In his will Hermann left a bequest of 75,000 gold marks (c. £700,000) to be shared between Jock and Richard. However, he stipulated that whilst Richard could inherit at the age of majority (twenty-one) Jock would have to wait until he was twenty-five because of his 'unsolid way of life'.[22] On his return to the UK in April 1901, Jock withdrew from the scheme and joined the Wilson Line based at Hull, as 4th Officer on the steamship *Lorenzo*.[23]

Now firmly based in the UK, Jock followed in the path of his Uncle Ernst, and in May 1902 sought naturalisation as a British citizen. By then he had built up the necessary years of UK qualifying residence, even though he had spent most of them at sea. His sponsors included James Culross and his friends in Harrogate, whom Jock would have met during his time between voyages to Australia. Documents were drawn up, memorials signed and the papers submitted to the Home Office by Jock's solicitor. Jock's application included a clue as to the next step in the life of this young man. He had been offered a commission in the 3rd Battalion of the East Yorkshire Militia Regiment, probably through connections he had made during his time in Harrogate.[24] The naturalisation process was completed and Jock took his oath of allegiance on 3 June 1902 as Otto Campbell Philippi, but he was commissioned into the militia on 11 June as 2nd Lt John Campbell.[25]

The change of name was sudden and one can only surmise the possible reasons. Jock had obviously decided on the name-change whilst going through the naturalisation process and before joining the militia. It is likely, therefore, to have been linked to his career change, combined with a wish to totally Anglicise himself. He had already used the Christian name James when joining the Merchant Navy as a runaway, and during the Brassey scheme period Jock, as Otto, may have been considered an outsider by the other British midshipmen. Furthermore, Kaiser Wilhelm and Otto von Bismark were, from the 1880s, a rich source for British cartoon satirists, so Jock's German heritage and his Christian name was potential ammunition for tormentors.

**'Jock', 2nd Lt J. Campbell,
East Yorkshire Militia Regiment, c. 1902**

It is unlikely that the reason was linked to his Jewish roots although it is odd that after the confirmation of Jock's naturalisation appeared in the *London Gazette* on 2 November 1902, it was picked up and published by the Jewish Chronicle in a list of Jews who had been granted British citizenship:[26] this despite Jock's ancestors converting to Lutheranism in the early 1800s. Whatever Jock's reasons for changing his name, it would complicate matters for future researchers.

Jock was based at Beverley in Yorkshire, whereas most of his 3rd Battalion had been posted to South Africa and were fighting in the Boer war. Those who remained and the new recruits were placed on garrison duty or exercises in Yorkshire. By this time, the twenty-two-year-old Jock was, because of the Brassey Scheme, more educated and worldly compared to the youth that had been rescued from Gloucester and taken to Largs. He was a young man, financially independent through the inheritance from his father's estate, handsome, fit, and with perfect written and spoken English, despite his German father. He had or was about to meet his wife to be, Aimee Dorothy Philips.

Aimee Dorothy Campbell (née Philips)

Dorothy had been living in Greenwich, London, with her parents until 1901, and it is possible that they met through one of Jock's naval instructors in the Brassey Scheme, who lived in their neighbourhood. In 1901 Dorothy's father, who had for many years worked for the Post Office, was promoted to Postmaster and Surveyor in Manchester, and that year the family moved north. They lived in a comfortable house in a middle-class area on the outskirts of Manchester, and in his new job John Philips was credited with starting up the 'Post Early for Christmas' campaign which he first trialled in Rochdale in 1902.[27]

Jock was, by now, widely travelled and had heard first-hand of the experiences of his Uncle Ernst setting up businesses in promising overseas markets, including Argentina. Jock's romantic idealism kicked in again. His wanderlust and adventurism, together with a sprinkling of Ernst's entrepreneurial spirit, sent him off from Southampton on 14 August 1903 for a fact-finding trip to Buenos Aires. Two days out Jock sent a cable back, from RMS *Thames*, to his fiancée, Dorothy, speaking of looking forward to their marriage and of listening out for fellow passengers who may be knowledgeable about Buenos Aires.[28] During their courtship, the possibility of a life in the Argentine must have been discussed; however, Dorothy was from a more protected background than Jock and may not have fully comprehended what sort of life lay ahead.

Jock returned to the UK on 9 November 1903 and, following the reading of the banns, he and Dorothy were married at St Gabriel's Parish Church, Hulme, Manchester, on the 15 December 1903. The witnesses were Dorothy's father, John Philips, and E. M. Cunninghame, probably Jock's best man, Lt Edward Montgomery-Cunninghame, of the Royal Horse Artillery, who had fought in the Boer War, and whose father was member of parliament for the area covering Largs, where Jock had stayed in 1897–98. In keeping with his new identity Jock gave his father's name, falsely, as Henry Campbell instead of Otto Heinrich Philippi: a pseudonym he would use for his father in future official documents. This supports the view that he had every intention of being taken as British, even though his new wife and in-laws would have known of his naturalisation.

Christmas celebrations, packing and family farewells followed, culminating in an 'At Home' party on 21 January 1904, hosted by John Philips, to celebrate his daughter's marriage to Jock.[29] Two weeks later, on 5 February 1904, the young couple set sail for their new life, initially in Buenos Aires, arriving in one of Argentina's hottest and most humid months. Dorothy may have found that Buenos Aires, in many respects, warranted its future reputation as the Paris of Latin America, but in the camp life was very different. This is where Jock sought his first investment, in an undeveloped area in Cordoba province, about two hundred miles north-west of Buenos Aires.

After some time in Buenos Aires and probably Rosario, which could be reached by train, Jock and Dorothy moved to the country. Jock had purchased a small parcel of land at San Antonio, near San Marcos, 110 miles west of Rosario. Another train line ran from Rosario to San Marcos, but from there Jock and Dorothy needed to ride to their farm some miles away. Because of the complete lack of infrastructure, early settlers had to live in mud huts until they were able to build their own property and little had changed by the time Jock arrived. This was the land of the gaucho and the mosquito.

Dorothy, unlike earlier settlers from sturdy Scottish farming stock, would not have experienced such deprivation, but set about supporting Jock in his venture. Their plot was not of sufficient size to run a commercial operation, but it would have provided Jock with an insight into managing livestock and his *peon* workers. Evidence of his struggle is found in the diary of John Benitz of Estancia Los Algarrobos, in an entry dated 25 March 1905, when he wrote,

> Mr J. Campbell took away 15 cart horses and 1
> mare, to his place in San Marcos, where he is to
> feed and gentle them for a month. We pay maize
> and one peon. He takes them to England to sell
> for our account. He to get 5% on the price fetched
> in England, all expenses for our account. He will
> bring out a thoroughbred stallion which we will
> buy and keep on halves. I to give the mares and he
> to feed and care for. [30]

It was not a large contract, but Jock was leveraging
his equine contacts in the UK and building connections
with the well-respected Benitz family. The Los Algarrobos
estate covered over 24,000 acres, with a main house of
twenty rooms and numerous estate buildings to support
the farm and its workers; amongst them, houses for the
mayordomo and his assistant, a butchery, food store,
stables, tack-room, and a place for the *peons* to drink *maté*.
The two-storey main house, with its colonnaded veranda
and balcony on three sides of the building, was set in an
oasis of trees and verdant lawns. This was a far cry from
Jock's humble 250 acres.

Dorothy returned to the UK in poor health and, in
May 1905, Jock wrote telling her that he had sold his
land and that he was concerned about the health of his
livestock.[31] In July, Dorothy returned to Argentina and
Jock's younger brother, Richard, sailed out from Hamburg
to join them. Jock had found a 1,623-acre *estancia* for sale
near Woodgate, twenty miles south of San Antonio, and it
was soon acquired by Jock and Richard. The cost of the
land was 44,000 pesos (c. £700,000), which was financed
from the brothers' bequest from their grandfather and a loan
from their Uncle Ernst. The newly purchased *estancia* was

renamed Los Dos Hermanos (the two brothers) and was a thirty-mile ride from the nearest train station at Leones, via a bridge across the Rio Terceiro.

The *estancia* house had been built in the European style by the previous owners, the Bocchi family. It was approached through large iron gates and a tree-lined avenue, providing an imposing entrance to the property. Additional trees within the compound gave much-needed protection against the summer heat. The house abutted a large barn (which included stabling), and additional buildings outside of the compound provided storage and/or accommodation for staff. It was a vast improvement on San Antonio.

Estancia Los Dos Hermanos, c. 1906

Later in 1905 Richard returned to resume his studies at Heidelberg University and from 1905 to 1910 Jock and Dorothy set about making the *estancia* a viable business. The couple's social life included spending time with landowners in the area and with other contacts in Rosario and Buenos Aires, where Jock also had a titular role with the La Plata Reel Cotton Company, a subsidiary of J. & P. Coats, set up by his Uncle Ernst. It was a hard life, but Jock and his

Doly-Booboo, as he called Dorothy, were young, newly married and sharing this adventure together. During this time they lived with a maid and a groom, and Jock, a gifted artist, captured examples of their life by drawing cartoons of his beloved Doly. From these cartoons, it is apparent that Dorothy was riding, shooting, driving a carriage and experiencing all aspects of life in the camp.

Dorothy Campbell and her cartoon 'Doly-Booboo'

Cartoon of 'Doly-Booboo' with groom Elias

Amongst their friends were engineers who were surveying and building an extension to the railroad, passing close to their land at Woodgate. When Jock and Dorothy arrived in 1905, the only building in Woodgate was a guesthouse, which in 1909 was sold or given to the railroad by the owner on condition that the location's name was changed to Monte Buey, the name of the guest house. In 1910 this house became the railway station and for a while remained the only building in town.

Jock and Dorothy were out of the country when the new Monte Buey station opened because during 1909 Dorothy became pregnant with their first child. Although she had embraced her life with Jock in the pampas it was not a place in which she wished to give birth to her children, especially as the baby was due in December, the hottest month of the year in Argentina. Consequently, in July 1909 Dorothy arrived back in the UK and made her way to her parents' house in Manchester. Jock followed, returning in time for the birth of Patrick on 24 December, which he duly registered the following January, giving his occupation as 'Farmer and Land Owner (Argentine)' and his address as the 'Junior Naval and Military Club, Piccadilly, London'.[32]

The following year Dorothy's father, John Philips, retired and moved, with his wife and daughter, Madeleine, to a large villa in a quiet tree-lined road in Buxton, Derbyshire. At the same time Jock rented a farmhouse, Pool Hall, in the village of Hartington in the Peak District, ten miles away from Dorothy's parents, and with a direct train line to Buxton. Here, Jock and Dorothy, together with their young groom, Elias Ferreyra, who had travelled back with Jock from Argentina, were joined by a locally-hired maid.

Hartington sits at the end of the Dove Valley and was surrounded by dairy herds, which provided milk for the creamery that at this time provided over 25 per cent of the world's supply of Stilton cheese. Hartington was the only location outside of the Vale of Belvoir that had the right to produce Stilton, due to an historical accident in 1900, when Thomas Nuttall, of Beeby, Leicestershire, took over the creamery in order to escape an outbreak of foot and mouth disease.

Here in the Derbyshire dales, during the summer of 1911, Dorothy and Jock's second child was conceived. Dorothy had her sister and parents living nearby for support and the couple were able to socialise with others in Hartington and the surrounding villages. The incumbent of St Giles' Church, the Revd James Rhodes Ashworth, and his family, who resided at the vicarage, were amongst their acquaintances. The reverend lived with his wife, Florence, and their two unmarried daughters, Sybil and Irene. Dorothy, a regular churchgoer and only a few years older than the daughters, would have undoubtedly had contact with them, as would Jock. Although in Jock's case, as is discovered later, such contact may have been closer than Dorothy would have wished.

For whatever reason, their time in Hartington was cut short and by the time their second child was born Jock and Dorothy had moved to The Mount in Quarndon, a few miles north of Derby. The Mount was owned by Capt. Lionel Guy Gisborne, who had for many years been with the Derbyshire Militia, and who could have become acquainted with Jock through hunting, the militia or their club in London. Jock's second son, Richard Michael, was born on 10 April 1912, yet Jock seems conspicuous by his absence. The birth was not registered until thirty-nine days later (forty-two days being the time limit for registration) by Dorothy. It is possible that Jock was spending more time away from his family at his club in London, as later correspondence indicates he was having an affair; a theme that continues for the remainder of Jock's life. Whilst Jock's charm, gregarious nature and artistic skills were all positive aspects of his character, his eye for the ladies would be his Achilles heel.

A few months later Jock and Dorothy moved again before Jock returned to his business interests in Argentina, sailing on the *Highland Piper* with his groom, Elias. The new family home was Coombe House, Uley, Gloucestershire, a beautiful early-Georgian clothier's house. Jock's hunting and militia contacts had come into play again, as the house was owned by the family of Jack Southwell Russell, the 25th Lord de Clifford, who had been killed in a motor car accident in Brighton in 1909, at the age of twenty-five. Russell had been a lieutenant in the Shropshire Yeomanry and also a hunter.

Jock's trip did not go well and in October he was holed up in the English Club, on the Calle 25 de Mayo in Buenos Aires, having been taken ill. For Jock, who typically embraced all things English, the club provided him with a familiar, male-only bastion similar to the environment of the Junior Naval and Military in London. With dark wood-panelled walls, a lounge dominated by a large painting of London, a bar pervaded by the aroma of cigars and a suite of rooms where members could stay, it was Jock's home from home. From the club, Jock wrote several letters to Dorothy and talked of being ill and thinking that he had had a stroke 'in this horrible country'.[33] Jock's enthusiasm for Argentina may have been beginning to wane, and would not have been helped by his illness and concerns about his relationship with Dorothy. He wrote lovingly to her, but acknowledged her awareness that, recently, there had been another woman in his life. Apparently the affair was now over and Dorothy had forgiven him. She sent a reply by Italian steamer, for speed of delivery, 'Courage, business nearly done then you can come home.'[34]

Jock returned from Argentina before the year was out and during the next six months had to seriously consider his future life with Dorothy and his possible love–hate relationship with Argentina. Both he and Dorothy had now fallen ill whilst in the Argentine, the *estancia* had not been a financial success, Jock was in discussion with Uncle Ernst regarding additional financing and they had two small sons to consider.

In the summer of 1913 Jock's stepfather was on a whale and polar bear hunting trip in the Arctic. Francis's passion for adventure, alluded to earlier, had led to him to become an expert in polar exploration. Such was his experience that in 1908, 1909 and 1910 he chartered the *Lofoten* out of Tromsø and arranged passenger cruises to the Arctic. In 1911 he submitted a proposal to the Royal Geographical Society in Madrid for a Spanish Polar Expedition which might take as long as five years. The plan was accepted and a new ship was commissioned. As he waited for her to be built, Francis had arranged his current hunting trip, chartering the *Fonix*, also out of Tromsø. He departed in July 1913 with two Scots, four other Spaniards, a captain and a Norwegian crew. Their adventure is recounted by one of the Scots, William Burn Murdoch, in *Modern Whaling and Bear Hunting*. The erudite, loquacious and mandolin-playing Francis de Gisbert discussed during the voyage the upcoming Spanish expedition, due to depart in 1915. It was agreed that Burn Murdoch, himself a polar explorer, would accompany the expedition as far as the Lena River delta, on another ship carrying Francis's wife, Mary, and their young daughter, also Mary.[35]

By the time Francis had completed the polar bear hunting trip and returned to Hamburg, Jock's deliberations over his future had been settled, at least temporarily. Jock, Dorothy and Patrick were to return to Argentina; Uncle Ernst was to provide additional funds, Jock having confirmed to him that Argentina is where they planned to remain, and surprisingly Michael was to remain in the UK in the care of Dorothy's mother and sister. It is difficult to comprehend the decision to leave one child behind or the reason for it, especially as during the next eighteen years that Jock maintained a home in the Argentine, Michael never once visited the country. Was Michael a weak child who could be not be risked in the heat and humidity? Was it an insurance policy for Dorothy: a reason to return to the UK, given the cracks in their relationship and possible second thoughts about *estancia* life?

Ernst sent Jock £150 (c. £10,000) to cover running expenses,[36] and on 11 September 1913 Jock sailed out of London on the *Highland Laddie*, together with Dorothy and Patrick, leaving the deteriorating political situation in Europe behind them. Argentina on the other hand was at the height of its so-called Golden Age, becoming the world's tenth leading economy, ahead of France and Germany. Buenos Ayres had, since the turn of the century, become more commonly known as Buenos Aires, and its epithet as the Paris of Latin America was well and truly cemented. Within a year it would have its own Harrods store, the only overseas branch of its London parent.

Jock and Dorothy resettled at Los Dos Hermanos, John Argentine was still playing first-class polo, and John Burnet was a stalwart of the Lomas cricket team. But events in Europe were about to change this status quo.

4

Return to the Old Country – WWI

The true soldier fights, not because of what is in front of him, but because he loves what is behind him.

G. K. Chesterton

H istorically, the impact of British immigrants on the business, sporting and social life in Argentina in general, and in Buenos Aires in particular, far outweighed that of other immigrant groups who measured a far greater number. They punched above their weight and this was to be the case during WWI. In the Argentine national census of May 1914 there were 28,300 British residents, i.e. those born in Great Britain, and many more who had been born in Argentina and whose parents or grandparents were British. Of these with a British heritage almost five thousand volunteered for service, over half of whom were, or became, officers.

The response of the British community in Buenos Aires to the declaration of war on 4 August 1914 was immediate.

Some reserve officers, who were able to sort out personal and private issues quickly, sailed for the UK three days later, and the first batch of 150 volunteers sailed out of Montevideo on 19 August. Many took longer to organise themselves. Some, despite being of war age, would declare themselves or be declared as unfit, some would remain to look after family business interests and others would become involved in the myriad of fundraising and support activities across Argentina. It is said that the majority of the British or their descendants did not see themselves as immigrants but merely as visitors to a foreign country, and this may go a long way to explaining the pull of their home country at a time of conflict.

John Argentine Campbell, despite being born in Argentina, illustrates this immediate response in a letter he wrote on 5 August 1914 to Lewis Lacey, a friend and fellow leading polo player, with whom he was due to play in the upcoming Argentine Open.

> Dear Lewis
>
> I have just heard that war is declared between England and Germany. Although possibly it may seem foolish, I would prefer not to play public polo while our people are at it over there; so I hope you will allow me to stand out. I feel that if one can go in for games at this time we shouldn't be here but should be on our way to the other side. What I hope is that the Almighty on whom that big German Emperor is always calling, will give the Germans such a hiding that they won't rise up again for another 100 years.
>
> Yours JAC
>
> ...will you tell Casares and Holway I am very sorry not to play with them. [1]

John Argentine and John Burnet Campbell, although born in the Argentine, would qualify as British subjects because their fathers were born in the UK, and John Otto was British by naturalisation. However, none were ordinarily resident in the UK and not obliged to return, and neither returned immediately to fight. They believed, as was the consensus at the time, that the war would end swiftly and decisively, in Britain's favour.

By 8 August the British Patriotic Committee had been formed in Buenos Aires. Their remit was to provide assistance to the families of reservists who were returning to the UK, to assist others affected by the war and to provide assisted passages to those who wished to volunteer, but were unable to pay their own way to the UK. However, underlying this formal purpose there existed an informal recruitment process. Informal because Argentina was a neutral country and 'care had to be taken to avoid infringement of neutrality laws'.[2]

The committee continued to provide a focus for British subjects throughout the war. It maintained a register of volunteers, provided free medicals for potential recruits prior to travel and liaised with the War Office in London. It also set up the Derby Register (Argentina) 1916, which recorded every British subject of military age (18–41) resident in Argentina, and issued exemption certificates to individuals whose work was indispensable to British and Allied interests in Argentina, or who were over age or unfit for service, or who had families dependent upon them.[3]

When volunteer recruitment dried up in the UK, the government enacted the Compulsory Military Service Act 1916, which created much interest in Buenos Aires. Although British residents in Argentina were not bound by any of its provisions, there was suddenly an increased desire from many who had previously found it impossible to get away, for well-founded reasons, to now offer their services.[4]

John Burnet Campbell (Jack) remained in Buenos Aires throughout the war. He was probably fit enough to join up, as he continued to play cricket until the 1920s and, despite being in his mid-thirties, his age would not have been a bar to active service. However, Jack's mother had died in 1907, his alcoholic father had slipped into a state of dementia and in 1912 he had become self-employed. Family responsibilities and a duty to his new business partner may well have precluded him from joining the war effort in the UK.

Although we do not know for certain, it is possible that Jack obtained an exemption certificate due to the possibility of serious hardship being caused by his business obligations and domestic situation. However, remaining at home during the conflict did not mean that he made no contribution to the war effort, as many who remained were involved in a host of charitable activities, from raising funds to supporting the families whose men had left for the front.

In Germany, Richard Philippi, the brother of John Otto Campbell, had completed his national service and was a reservist; at the outbreak of war he was immediately called into the 18th Reserve Corps at Frankfurt. His unit joined the German IV Army under Generaloberst Albrecht, Duke of Wurttemberg and was despatched to the Ardennes in Belgium. The French became aware of the gathering German forces and, on 20 August 1914, Commander-in-Chief Joffre authorised the French forces to move in for an attack. In the woods of the Ardennes, on a foggy 21 August, the opposing troops chanced upon each other, and sporadic fighting broke out. The following day a bloody battle was fought near Neufchateau, during which Richard, who was with the Artillery Munitions Column attached to the 18th Reserve Corps, was hit by gunfire. The French forces retreated on 23 August and Unteroffizier Richard Philippi, who had been lightly wounded, was sent home. His war was over within the first month of what would become a long and extremely grim conflict. This would signal the start of the pain and turmoil suffered by Jock's relatives, whose family members were fighting on opposing sides of the war.

The extended Philippi family were wealthy and educated and by 1914 were also geographically widespread, living in the USA, the UK and Germany. Jock's great-uncle Eduard had moved to the UK in 1840s, and his Aunt Magda was living in England with her husband, Ernst. When war broke out family members not only found themselves in the wrong country, but some were also conscripted to fight against each other.

Ernst and Magda's children, because of Ernst's British naturalisation, joined the British Army, whereas the couple's nephews fought for the Germans. Jock's maternal aunts had all been born in Hamburg and were now married and living in England, but their brother had remained in Hamburg as a naturalised German. The same applied to Jock and his brother, Richard, who had remained in Germany. These interwoven relationships created difficult emotions and tensions between country and kin, which became unbearable as the war progressed.

The situation regarding Jock's mother and her second husband was also complicated. She was British, although she had been born in Germany, and Francis had dual nationality because his father was Spanish and his mother English. Francis had been making the final plans for the Spanish Polar Expedition but, following the outbreak of war, it was cancelled. Once war had been declared, some British subjects returned immediately to the UK whilst those who remained could be interned in Germany or sent home. Mary and Francis probably decided to move immediately to the UK and bought a house in Ponteland, outside of Newcastle, close to where Francis's father had lived and where they would spend the rest of their lives. Francis was too old for active service in the British Army, and instead volunteered to work in a munitions factory.[5]

The war did not end as quickly as envisaged, and Jock, having possibly been contacted by the British Patriotic Committee, made his way to Buenos Aires for a medical examination. He passed and cabled ahead to let his hunting friend Russell Monro, who was at Llandrindod Wells taking a cure for his gout, know that he was about to leave Buenos Aires and on arrival would make his way directly to the War Office in London. Russell wrote to his contact at the War Office to pass on the message, to remind him that Jock was to join the Royal Field Artillery (RFA) and to vouch for him.

On 25 May 1915 Jock arrived at Liverpool with Dorothy and Patrick, on the *Darro*. Jock and his family made their way to London; Jock to the Junior Naval and Military Club on Piccadilly, where he was to stay, Dorothy and Patrick to be reunited with Michael before making their way, eventually, to Pond Cottage on the Crawley Court estate. Leaving Argentina, having only recently returned after the births of their children, must have been a wrench for the family. However, for Jock the return to join the war may have been less difficult. As a naturalised British subject, an anglophile and with a previous army commission, it seems likely that he would have wanted to serve rather than be coerced. Also Jock, who was a romantic and an adventurer, as shown by his time in the Brassey Scheme and his enthusiastic migration to Argentina, would, like many others of the officer class, see the war as a game, a bit of sport, a jolly jape. They would all, sooner or later, become disabused of that notion.

On 26 May Jock enlisted and the following day Russell Monro, having returned from Llandrindod Wells, signed Jock's certificate of good character within his enlistment papers. Having previously been an officer with the militia, Jock may have foregone some of the basic military training but would have still attended one of the fast-track RFA officer training units. He passed out as 2nd Lt J. Campbell, RFA, and was assigned to the 166th Brigade, a newly formed unit. The 166th was one of many artillery brigades that formed part of the 33rd Division of Kitchener's Fourth New Army. This division of locally raised soldiers became known as the 'Pals', as it comprised groups of young men known to each other from public schools, boy's brigades, football teams, employment, etc.

In the summer of 1915 the various units within the 33rd Division, including Jock's 166th Brigade, massed at Clipstone, near Mansfield, for the start of a more cohesive divisional training programme. By the end of the year they were in France for final training, but it would be many more months before they would move to the front, and even then there was only sporadic action. His Pals brigade consisted mostly of new recruits, without any war or even army experience, but as they emerged from the cold and miserable winter their proximity and training over the past months had, at least, bonded them as a team, which would become crucial. The brigade had four batteries, each commanded by a major, and each battery had around a hundred and eighty officers and men covering three sections, each with two guns. Jock, now promoted to the temporary rank of lieutenant, led one of these sections, commanding twenty men. Supporting each battery was a veritable industry of horses, drivers, farriers, wheelers and quartermasters.

'Jock', 2nd Lt J. Campbell,
Royal Field Artillery, c. 1915

After a quiet start to his war Jock was, in May 1916, finally in action at Annequin, close to Bethune on the La Bassée front. This was a holding front, not considered large-scale action, and therefore perfect for training the raw 33rd Artillery Division. Nevertheless, here the brigade came under regular shelling attacks and suffered their first casualties. Jock was witnessing for the first time the explosions of his own guns, firing in anger, and the whooshing sound of incoming shells, followed by a thud and an immediate explosion. Whilst Jock's mind was on managing his gun section, his unconscious was playing a game of Russian roulette with enemy shells heading in his direction.

The brigade was relieved at the end of May, but instead of moving out, Jock was transferred to the HQ staff of 167th Brigade and endured a further five weeks dug in at the front. The formation of the division had recently been modified, moving from three brigades of 18-pounder guns and one brigade of 4.5-inch howitzers to four brigades each with both guns, in order to provide more flexibility. It is possible that this reorganisation led to Jock's transfer to HQ as he had been in control of two 18-pounders, within D battery, which would have become the 166th Brigade's howitzer battery. It is also possible that Jock's character was identified as having the qualities necessary to become an Orderly Officer, responsible for stores, transport and discipline. His gregarious character and experience of managing subordinates in adverse conditions whilst in the Brassey Scheme would have been ideal for managing the interface between the supply lines, the Commanding Officer and the gunner ranks. However, being a Brigade HQ staff officer did not mean Jock was immune from enemy attack as he was usually situated within yards of the gun batteries.

On 6 July the remaining brigades of the 33rd Divisional Artillery on the La Bassée front received orders to move out within eleven hours and start their journey south, to the terrifying Battle of the Somme. This would have been a major logistical problem for Jock, but he accomplished it in the allotted time. There was some respite for the men on their way south, but not for Jock as he arranged for train transportation and found billeting areas for almost eight hundred men, six hundred horses, guns and ammunition. As the brigade marched the last leg of their journey to the Somme, chaos, noise and smells enveloped the men: the constant boom of artillery fire in the distance, the eye-watering effect of the gas from the lachrymose shells drifting across the fields towards them, the continuous horse-drawn train of supplies to the front, and the haunted look of soldiers slowly returning back through the line for treatment or rest.

Ten days after leaving La Bassée they were settled in the area just to the east of Mametz Wood, from where the brigade were able to provide additional artillery support for the ongoing nightmare battle for High Wood. Jock would not emerge unscarred. He was now witnessing the horror of almost stalemate trench warfare, as the front line had only edged forward by yards, rather than miles, over the previous months. The adjacent Mametz Wood had only been taken a few days before Jock had arrived and the action, including hand-to-hand fighting, had lasted five days. The writer and poet Robert Graves had taken part in the attack as an infantry officer, and on returning to the wood, immediately after the battle had been won, recalled, 'It was full of dead Prussian Guards Reserve, big men, and dead Royal Welch and South Wales Borderers of the New Army battalions, little men. Not a single tree in the wood remained unbroken.'[6] Captain Graves was then ordered to move forward for an attack on High Wood during which he was severely wounded. So bad was his condition that as he was removed from the field his Commanding Officer, assuming he would die of his wounds, wrote to Graves' parents that he had died. Graves survived and was back at the front in 1917.

For the next three weeks, Jock endured almost daily enemy shell and gas attacks whilst his brigade bombarded High Wood to soften up the Germans in advance of an all-out infantry attack. On occasions the British shelling was incessant, with all guns firing at a rate of one round per minute. Under these conditions, one battery could use as much ammunition in twenty-four hours as a whole brigade had used in a week at the less-demanding La Bassée front. By now the Germans had a good fix on the location of the British artillery positions and on 21 July enemy shells landed on the road close to Jock's HQ, cutting off 167th Brigade's communications. A barrage of tear and poisonous gas shells followed and the next day the Brigade HQ was almost wiped out when a heavy German shell landed nearby, and in a deafening explosion wounded a regimental sergeant major and driver and killed a horse.

The story was the same for the remainder of the month as the HQ came under attack again and again from both explosive and gas shells and it could not have been any worse for Jock than if he had remained with his gun section. When the brigade was finally relieved on 11 August and moved out to rest, the battle for High Wood was still raging. Jock had been at or near the front for more than three months: an unusually long stint. Both soldiers and officers tried to recover from the after-effects, including deafness, lack of sleep, malnourishment, nightmares and flashbacks, but again Jock's period of recovery was short-lived.

After five days his brigade were once more ordered to prepare for action. However, in this instance, apart from moving from one billet to another, there was none.

On 11 September Jock's commanding officer, Lt-Col. Stewart, was posted to 166th Brigade and took Jock with him as his HQ Orderly Officer. Jock was not only returning to his original brigade, but also back to Mametz Wood, where the 166th were still supporting the ongoing attempt to secure High Wood: a battle which would not be settled until 15 September, after a huge loss of life on both sides. Stories later emerged of trenches being protected by the bodies of dead soldiers packed high and covered with earth, only to be once again blown apart by a subsequent attack. Thousands of bodies of British and German soldiers were never recovered from High Wood.

Jock, not being an infantry officer, escaped the immediacy of hand-to-hand combat and trench warfare, but not the aftermath. At the time that High Wood was secured, only four days after Jock had arrived back at Mametz, his brigade was relieved. Jock was by now beginning to suffer from the trauma of war and was granted a short leave back to the UK, although he did not meet his family. It is possible that this time away from the discipline of the army and the now familiar sounds and smells of destruction had a negative effect on him, making any future return to the front even more difficult.

By 5 October Jock was back in action, but his letters to Dorothy, later in the month, highlight his deteriorating state of mind. The first talked of being 'once more in the thick of it'[7] and how the shelling made him nervous, and the second again complained of his nerves. Letters were censored during the war and stamped by an officer in the regiment before their release. As well as censoring information about troop movements, the War Office was also anxious that letters did not contain negative descriptions about the horrors of war, as such detail might dissuade others from joining up. Many soldiers used self-censorship in this regard in order not to distress their loved ones and some avoided censorship altogether, by asking another soldier returning home on leave to post a letter in the UK.

On 15 November Jock wrote once more to Dorothy, hoping that his previous letter had not frightened her. However, later in the letter, he reiterated that his nerves were bad and said that he feared 'falling to pieces'.[8] Both his need to confide in and to burden Dorothy and the regularity of the letters suggests an open and trusting relationship with his wife, but may also allude to Jock's selfishness. On 19 November the 166th Brigade marched out and away from the conflict to the safety of the wagon lines. For Jock, whose condition continued to deteriorate, the war had ended. On 1 December he was admitted to a field hospital and then, on 5 December, was shipped back to England from Le Havre.

A week later John Argentine Campbell was also returning to the UK from the front line in France, but under entirely different circumstances. He had been granted special leave of ten weeks in order to return to Buenos Aires to undertake some urgent private business. He made his way to his sister Leila's house at Eastbourne, where he spent Christmas with his wife Myra, their children and Leila's family. Myra and John then travelled to Liverpool, where, on 29 December 1916, they set sail on the SS *Drina*, a Royal Mail Packet Steamer, bound for Buenos Aires. The *Drina* was a large luxurious ship, with accommodation for 200 first-class passengers, 50 second-class and 1,200 in steerage. In 1914 she had been commandeered for use as a hospital ship, but returned in 1916 to trade and passenger transport routes.

John's war had also been delayed, possibly due to the health of his father and concerns over the management of the La Corona and El Jabali estates. John's father died at La Corona on 11 June 1915 and John, having sorted out the affairs of his father and prepared his will, planned for his return to the UK. Earlier, in February, Kaiser Wilhelm had announced a German naval blockade of UK waters and although it was immediately lifted, following a complaint by the United States, John would not have wanted to risk his family's safety and arranged to travel separately. His concern was a valid one, as he and Myra discovered fourteen months later.

John sailed ahead in October, via Madeira, and arrived in Liverpool on 1 November 1915. Despite having given his UK address as that of his sister, Leila, he made his way directly to London. Myra followed several days later, together with their three children, Roderick, Tony and Joan, arriving at the safer destination of Falmouth, in the south of England. From there they travelled to Eastbourne, with Myra travelling on alone to be with John at the Hyde Park Hotel on Knightsbridge, in London.

The hotel had originally been a gentleman's club, but following a fire in 1899 it reopened in 1902 as the grandest hotel in London. The original club entrance faced Hyde Park, but as a hotel it was moved to the Knightsbridge side because Queen Victoria dictated that no advertising should face a royal park. This rule remains to this day in the revamped and renamed Mandarin Oriental Hyde Park Hotel, where only royalty or those with the permission of the royal household can use the Albert Gate entrance on the park side. Here Myra and John could enjoy each other's company whenever John was able to take time out from his training.

John had reached London and enlisted, having been vouched for by General Rimington, Commander of the Indian Cavalry Corps and ex 6th Inniskilling Dragoon officer, with whom John had become acquainted through polo circles. On 3 November John was posted to the 2nd HQ Reserve Cavalry Regiment at Aldershot Barracks, where he commenced his officer training. During the next three months John had the opportunity to see his wife and children in London or Eastbourne before completing his training and passing out as 2nd Lt J. A. Campbell.

**John Argentine, 2nd Lt J. A. Campbell,
6th Inniskilling Dragoons, c. 1915**

On 17 February 1916 John made his way to Folkestone
and was ferried to Boulogne en route to the theatre of war
and the Battle of the Somme. He joined his regiment,
the 6th Inniskilling Dragoons, at Feuquieres-en-Vimeu,
fourteen miles south-west of Abbeville, France, where they
were training. During the next few days, John, as a Scottish
rugby international, would have taken great interest, or
even participated, in three rugby matches against other
regiments, all which were won by the Inniskilling Dragoons.
As training continued, John became acquainted with his
regiment, known as the 'Skins', which was one of the most
famous cavalry units of the British Army; it had fought
with distinction at the Battle of the Boyne (1690) and the
Battle of Balaclava (1854). The history and pride of the
Inniskillings would have been even more apparent to John
when, on Sunday, 2 April, the regiment held a memorial
service for Captain Lawrence Oates to commemorate the
day he sacrificed his life for others. Oates had been an officer
in the Skins and after leaving the army he joined Scott on
his expedition to the South Pole. Although successful in
reaching the pole, they became bogged down in blizzardous
conditions on the return journey, and a severely frostbitten
Oates walked out into the night, not wishing to be a burden
to his colleagues. The regiment, now merged with the Royal
Dragoons, continues to hold these memorial services each
year on the Sunday closest to 16 March.[9]

For the remainder of April and through to September,
John moved with his regiment from camp to camp, and
apart from occasional working parties the regiment did little
but train as they waited to be called into action. At the end
of September, having received the order to advance, the
Skins arrived at Waterlot Farm, less than a couple of miles

away from where Jock had seen action in the previous year's July attack on High Wood. For the remainder of the year, John was involved in some relatively small skirmishes and more training before being granted his extended leave.

On 26 January 1917 the *Drina* docked in Buenos Aires and the next day the Buenos Aires *Standard* carried the notice that 'Mr & Mrs J. A. Campbell arrived at the Plaza Hotel yesterday.'[10] Intriguingly, in its Telefonia column the *Standard* carried a further notice on Sunday, 28 January, which read 'Mr John Argentine Campbell, the well known *estanciero* and sportsman who has been on the fighting land in France for nearly a year obtained special leave and arrived in this country by the *Drina* on an urgent business visit. He returns on the same steamer on 1 February.'[11] This is intriguing because whatever his private business was, it had to be accomplished in less than four working days, and it must have been urgent, because the army granted an extraordinary extended special leave and John had risked taking Myra on the journey with him. It is possible that it related to the transfer of his late father's estate or problems with one or both of the *estancias* now under his control. John duly left Argentina a few days later on the *Drina*, giving him a month to contemplate his return to the front as he relaxed on board with his wife.

On 1 March the steamship was on the last leg of her voyage to Liverpool, moving northwards, only two to three miles out from the Welsh coast, when an explosion rocked the ship. It was 11.57 p.m. and John and Myra had probably retired to bed, for what would have been their last night together. The ship had been holed, was taking in water and within minutes the captain had sounded the alarm and ordered passengers to make for the lifeboats. At 12.45 a.m.

on 2 March, during the ship's evacuation, there was a second explosion and the ship became fatally stricken and proceeded to sink.

The German U-boat UC65, under the command of Otto Steinbrink, had caused the damage by delivering two torpedoes into the *Drina*. Luckily, the sea was calm and very few of the crew and none of the passengers perished, with the survivors making landfall at Milford Haven. News of this sinking did not make the UK press at the time because of censorship, though the British War Cabinet minutes did note the loss. However, on Sunday, 4 March, the *Standard* in Buenos Aires announced that the SS *Drina* had been sunk, but that all passengers had made it safely to shore. The article went on to list sixty-seven passengers from Buenos Aires who had been saved, and first on the list were Mr & Mrs J. A. Campbell.[12]

According to the *Buenos Aires Herald*, the ship had been carrying a large cargo of frozen meat and coffee from Brazil, which, because these were classed as supplies, made it a valid target for the German Navy.[13] John must have been devastated for his wife to have witnessed and been involved in such an attack. Although she was a strong and possibly unemotional woman, just over a year earlier John had tried to protect her from such an attack by sending her separately to a port in the south of England. Now, as he was about to leave her to return to the Somme, their last few hours together had been overshadowed. Remarkably, within another week John was back with his regiment, but not before, according to family legend, Myra, who had lost all of her luggage, had been bought a new fur coat and a string of pearls, which were, in John's words, 'basic necessities'.[14]

When John reached his regiment on 9 March 1917 he discovered that neither the routine nor the battle lines had changed. It was a war of attrition, the like of which had never before been witnessed. On Sunday, 18 March, John attended the now-familiar Oates memorial service and the next day the regiment began their march towards the front line, only to be ordered to return to their previous camp at Miraumont. This action and inaction continued for most of the year, as had been the case in 1916. Short periods of dismounted attacks and trench warfare were followed by training and patrols and yet more training.

The only major event, during this time, meriting more than the odd word in the regiment's war diaries was an inspection by HRH the Duke of Connaught, Colonel in Chief of the 6th Inniskilling Dragoons. On 28 June 1916 a rehearsal was held, followed the next day by the inspection itself. HRH was complimentary regarding the appearance of the regiment, and remarked that he felt sure that when the opportunity arose the Skins 'would uphold the honour gained in the past'.[15] John may have missed the inspection, though it is more likely that he arrived back in the nick of time from a short leave to Paris. The reason behind the leave to Buenos Aires remains a mystery, but whilst he was in Paris John, on 26 June, signed a new will at the Ritz Hotel on Place Vendôme, replacing the one he had made in 1915 before joining up. The original 1915 will is lost and therefore it is not possible to know what had changed and why, but the trip to Argentina earlier in the year may have been related.

The regiment had spent most of July to November continually training at camps in and around Ennemain, and although this lack of action may have been frustrating, the use of cavalry, against the more-modern weapons being employed at that time, was becoming a rarity and only a few mounted charges were to take place during the remainder of the war. However, the Skins' time had come and whilst frustrations may have been relieved over the next few days the futility and errors of war would become only too apparent. On 30 November they moved out of Ennemain as cavalry and rode towards the hamlet of St Emilie. That evening the army commanders met to plan a counter-attack in the area around Villers-Guislain.

The attack, which would involve mounted cavalry supported by tanks, was planned for 6.30 a.m. the following day. John's dragoons, together with the 2nd Lancers of the Mhow Brigade (Indian Army), would be tasked with taking Villers Ridge east of Villers-Guislain, whilst the Lucknow Brigade and the 5th Cavalry were to attack Villers-Guislain itself. However, the expected tank support did not materialise and very quickly the attack on Villers-Guislain became bogged down amongst existing British-held trenches. Despite being prepared for action from 6.30 a.m., the 2nd Lancers and the Skins were not given the order to attack by their commanders, who were aware of the lack of tank support. At 7.45 a.m. the over-riding Cavalry Corp Commander, Lt-Gen. Kavanagh, having been told of this lack of movement, conferred with his hesitant commanders, and after a very short discussion ordered them to make the mounted attack. The cavalry commanders, despite knowing that such action was foolhardy, were forced to commit to the attack without the expected tank cover. At 8.15 a.m. the order was given 'to endeavour to push towards your objective supported by the artillery'.[16]

The 2nd Lancers formed up south of Peiziere, near Epèhy, and moved off at 9 a.m. supported by C Squadron of the Inniskilling Dragoons and a brigade machine-gun section. They advanced along the road north-east from Epèhy and, with pennanted lances drawn, broke into a gallop down the Catelet Valley. They immediately encountered machine-gun fire but managed to retake Kildare Trench, which had previously been held by the British. Though they then became bogged down for the remainder of the day.

The remaining Skins' squadrons, A, B and D, were unaware of the fate of the Lancers, and on seeing them move off earlier started their own advance. Setting out from the north-west of Peiziere, the formation was led by D Squadron, which included John, under the command of Captain Bridgewater. Without the acceleration of polo ponies, the cavalry's large steeds cantered off slowly and gathered speed before breaking into a gallop. Once committed to the charge and into open territory the dragoon squadrons, sabres in hand and rifles shouldered, came under heavy machine-gun fire from the German lines on their flank. As the gunfire wreaked havoc amongst the charging squadrons, John, fuelled with adrenaline and with senses heightened, probably faced the inevitable calmly. Horses fell from under their riders and lay whinnying and snorting in distress; cavalrymen were shot and left without cover or assistance and chaos ensued. Despite the hopelessness of the task, the survivors of D Squadron pushed on at a gallop whilst the two rear squadrons, witnessing the mayhem, were able to pull up and withdraw to Peiziere.

John, with the remainder of D Squadron and the machine-gun section, charged on towards their target. However, on reaching a sugar beet factory, they ran into

German reinforcements and a close-quarter fight began, during which Captain Bridgwater was killed. The skirmish did not last long; John was severely wounded in the side and the dragoons were forced to surrender. The prisoners were taken back behind the lines and John, bleeding profusely, was taken with the other wounded to a field hospital. Within ten minutes, in an action that was doomed before it started, the dragoons lost 102 men and 150 horses, and the machine-gun section of 55 men and 87 horses were all lost.

The fact that most, if not all, leading this attack were either killed or taken prisoner resulted in a paucity of information flowing back from the front. On 6 December 1917 a telegram from the War Office arrived at the Hans Crescent Hotel in London addressed to Mrs J. A. Campbell. 'Regret to inform you that Lt J. A. Campbell 6 Inniskilling Dragoons reported missing December past. This does not necessarily mean killed or wounded. Further news sent immediately rec'd.'[17]

Fearing the worst, yet hoping for good news, Myra Campbell remained at the hotel, but towards the end of January 1918 her hopes were dashed in the cruellest of fashions. Mrs Niall, the wife of 2nd Lt Niall, from the same squadron as John, received a postcard from her husband. The card included the words 'poor Campbell died of his wounds, let Roy [Mrs Niall's brother] know'.[18]

Myra, after receiving the tragic news from Mrs Niall, approached the War Office through her solicitor to obtain a death certificate, in order to begin the process of closing the affairs of her late husband. The War Office eventually received a letter from a Corporal Bird, who had witnessed John being wounded, thus corroborating the postcard information. This was followed by receipt of the official

5

Jock's Demise

*In wealth, many friends; in poverty, not
even relatives.*

Japanese proverb

On 7 December 1916 John Otto Campbell arrived at Dover and was transported to the Kitchener Hospital in Brighton. Originally the Elm Grove workhouse, it had been transformed into one of the many wartime hospitals scattered across the country. After being assessed and diagnosed with neurasthenia, more commonly known as shell shock, Jock was transferred to the Edward VII Convalescent Home for Officers, on the Isle of Wight, and granted leave from active service until 24 January. Although the assessors appeared optimistic that a return to the front line was realistic, Jock had been brought low by witnessing the horrors of artillery and trench warfare.

The convalescent home was situated in the subsidiary wings of Osborne House, originally Queen Victoria's holiday retreat, which had, upon her death, become a naval college.

Jock could have been suffering from any combination of symptoms associated with neurasthenia: restlessness, anxiety, nervous tics and nightmares. Robert Graves, the poet, who convalesced at Osborne House several months later, notes in his autobiography that 'many of the patients at Osborne were neurasthenic and should have been in a special neurasthenic hospital'.[1] Graves seems to suggest that those suffering from neurasthenia were, physically and mentally, in a worse condition than himself and others who had been hospitalised and were now convalescing.

Shell shock was becoming a more accepted condition within the armed services medical community. However, it was handled differently between officers and the ranks, with the latter often being accused of using it as an excuse, and in a few cases being shot for desertion. Also, the perceived wisdom in relation to officers was that a period of convalescence, away from home, speeded their recovery and enabled them to return more quickly to the front. Jock, either by using his persuasive charm or because Osborne House needed the bed, was discharged and allowed home on 14 December. Home was with his family, who were then gathering for Christmas at his Uncle Ernst's estate at Crawley. There he joined Dorothy and his children, who were staying at Pond Cottage, a beautiful thatched estate house.

The joy of being reunited with family was tempered by the sombre mood at Crawley Court. Jock was unwell and the impact of the war on Ernst and Magda was taking its toll. Magda had never completely recovered from the death of her daughter Kate in 1903, at the age of nine, and now she was faced with the horror of family members, in both Germany and the UK, fighting on opposite sides in a bloody war of attrition. Richard, Jock's brother, had already been injured at the very start of the war and now Jock was back from the front a broken man: temporarily at least.

Pond Cottage, Crawley Court Estate

Life for Ernst and Magda had also been soured by the way that the public and, more surprisingly, the management of J. & P. Coats, had turned against Ernst as the war progressed. At the outbreak of war he had founded a small hospital in Winchester for wounded soldiers and both of his sons were in the British Army.[2] The animosity towards naturalised Britons of German extraction generally, and towards his family in particular, hurt Ernst deeply, and in 1915 he was moved to respond, in a letter to the editor of the Hampshire Chronicle.[3]

SIR, —As the loyalty of naturalized British subjects and their views concerning the war have been called into question, I shall be glad if you will publish the following statement:-

There is no doubt in my mind that the responsibility for the war rests on Germany, and that for many years past she planned it and prepared for it. Whilst hoping that Great Britain would hold aloof for at least a time, the destruction of British sea power was the real objective of a war deliberately forced upon France and Russia when the time was thought propitious.

Certain methods of warfare to which Germany has resorted are so inhuman and wicked that they disgrace those who are responsible for them. Those with whom I am personally acquainted know that I have all along held and expressed these views. My two sons are both in the Army.

I was born in Prussia, but came to this country before I was of age. 48 years ago I was, at my request, released from my allegiance as a Prussian subject. Five years later I became a naturalized British subject. I have submitted to Major St. A. B. Warde, the Chief Constable of Hampshire, my certificate of naturalization and a document issued by the Prussian Ministry of the Interior on 8th March, 1867, to the effect that I had ceased on that day to be a Prussian subject.

Yours, &c., E. Philippi
Crawley, near Winchester, 19th May, 1915.

Ernst's resignation from J. & P. Coats followed in 1916, as anti-German pressure increased within the company.

Christmas and New Year had passed at Crawley and Jock's leave was nearing its end. On 19 January, having not heard from the army, he wrote saying that his leave was about to expire and that he was awaiting orders. Since the New Year, Magda's condition had worsened and faced with Jock's imminent departure from the safety of Crawley to return to the front, she passed away on 22 January. Her death caused the heartbroken Ernst to inscribe on her headstone a quote from Jeremiah 31:3, 'I have loved thee with an everlasting love, therefore with loving kindness I have drawn thee.'[4] It was a burden he was unable to carry for long, and on 11 February, less than a month after her death, Ernst succumbed to a heart attack.

During his time with J. & P. Coats, Ernst had transformed its international business and become a main board director involved in its flotation on the UK stock exchange. In the process he had amassed a fortune which at today's value would be in excess of £10 million. At J. & P. Coats' AGM, later in 1917, its chairman, in a pointed reference to the Germanophobes within his company, remarked,

> He has been taken away, dying very suddenly a few weeks after his wife's decease, his last days, I fear, embittered by the horrors of the war and the unjust suspicion of ignorant and narrow-minded individuals who did not know the real man. To those intimately acquainted with him he was known to be a loyal supporter of his adopted country.[5]

After Magda's death, Jock's leave had been extended and unsurprisingly it was further extended to 5 March after Ernst's passing. Having witnessed so much death and destruction in the field, Jock now, in the middle of his recuperative leave, had to cope with the loss of both his aunt and uncle, who had shown him so much kindness and support in the past. When he finally attended a Medical Board assessment on 26 March 1917, he was declared permanently unfit for further service of any kind. He subsequently resigned his commission, due to ill health, and on leaving the army was granted the honorary rank of lieutenant.

It is difficult to contemplate Jock's state of mind during the summer of 1917. Apart from the ongoing symptoms of his neurasthenia, Jock was possibly suffering from feelings of guilt and worthlessness at not having withstood the mental stress of war and may, like many others invalided out of the army, have wished that he had been killed in action rather than living in his current state. Jock decided to return to Argentina, but being of German birth and despite being naturalised he required War Office permission to travel. This was forthcoming on 23 July and Jock sailed back alone to Buenos Aires, aboard the *Amazon*, on 21 September.

Jock's reasons for travelling back on his own are unclear; his relationship with Dorothy may have deteriorated; she may have remained to be near the children as they started at preparatory school; he may have needed time on his own to rebuild his life and pride in Argentina, or perhaps it was related to his decision to sell Los Dos Hermanos. Travelling back alone and without continuing medical or family support may have been a risk given the long-term effects of his illness, which could have resulted in personality changes, including aggression, mood swings, anger, impulsiveness and loss of social judgment, some of which may explain Jock's behaviour towards the end of his life.

In January 1918 he was indeed taken ill at Los Dos Hermanos, suffering from a fever, being looked after by staff and pining for Dorothy to join him. He had already made the decision to sell the farm and move to Tucumán province, as his army records gave his forwarding address as Alpachiri, Concepción, Tucumán or the English Club, Buenos Aires. His main contacts near Alpachiri were the Carlisles, who owned Ingenio La Corona, a large sugar factory on the outskirts of Concepción, and Stewart Shipton, its factory manager. On 7 July Jock watched Carlisle and Shipton play polo and on 9 July he set out to visit Shipton's *estancia* and gauge the local camps. Jock was still looking at farms to buy, but had been frustrated by their owners' unwillingness to name a reasonable price. He was concentrating on properties in the foothills of the Aconquija mountains, west of Alpachiri and twelve miles from Concepción.

Dorothy and Patrick finally joined Jock in Argentina in June 1919, sailing out on the *Highland Pride* from London. Little is known about the family's time together in 1919–20, but it did not last long, and was obviously not a success in terms of their relationship, as Dorothy moved on to Rio de Janeiro, Brazil. There, Dorothy could seek comfort from her brother, Commander Christopher Hooper Philips, who was based in South America with the Royal Navy. In March 1920 Dorothy sent a short note to Jock, whose response was to plead for her to return: 'Come back to me soon my own Doly – don't lecture me when you do – let all be forgotten and don't nag me and you'll find in me (rotten as I am) your real lover.'[6] Jock had been caught out or admitted an affair around 1912, and it appears that he may have had other dalliances in the intervening years. Now he had been found out yet again and for Dorothy it was the final straw. With Jock's pleading falling on deaf years, Dorothy returned to the UK.

At the same time Jock received a curt letter from his brother, Richard, asking for his share of the proceeds from the sale of Los Dos Hermanos. Jock, having been remiss at not sending the proceeds earlier, immediately wired the money to Richard in Germany, and also repaid his uncle's loan to Ernst's children in the UK. The timing was not good, as Jock was close to consummating a deal to buy some land.

Jock's friend Stewart Shipton had become the first mayor of Concepción when it had been granted city status in 1901 and was well respected in the area. Besides his home in Concepción, Shipton also owned land in the mountains west of Alpachiri, including a *puesto* called La Cascades, north of the Rio Las Pavas. The area was rich in timber and Shipton would often spend weekends at La Cascades felling trees and enjoying the abundant wildlife. The land that Jock had identified lay adjacent to Shipton's, but south of the Las Pavas. It started at the confluence of the rivers Las Pavas and del Conventillo, six miles west of Alpachiri, and rose up through lush woodland between the two rivers. It continued above the tree line, into the barren reaches of the Aconquija mountains, ending at the snow-covered border of the Tucumán and Catamarca Provinces. At its highest, Jock's land stood over 16,000 feet above sea level, and situated at 13,000 feet were the ruins of the Inca settlement La Ciudacita (city on high). Having repaid his brother and cousins, Jock was forced to borrow to buy the land and in June 1920 he agreed a mortgage with his friend Shipton for 70,000 pesos (c. £340,000) to be repaid in seven years.[7] Jock was now Shipton's neighbour, and his well-stocked forest formed the basis for his next venture as a timber merchant.

Patrick started at Blundell's School, in Dorset, in September 1920 and Dorothy, with no significant financial support from Argentina, accepted help from Ernst's children to fund her children's school fees. By the time Michael joined Patrick at Blundell's, in 1921, Jock's status in the school register had changed from landowner to timber merchant, confirming Jock's new occupation.

Jock often stayed in the mountains at La Mesada, a *puesto* situated at 1,650 metres, on the trail leading to La Ciudacita. This area in Tucumán province, in particular Jock's land, is associated with natural beauty, legends and mythology, and Jock would have at some point investigated the extent of his domain by trekking, by pony, high into the mountains. He would have come across the Incan ruins, which, together with local folklore, may have been the catalyst for him to write a story for his niece Edina, in Germany. *A Tale of Inca Times* was written and illustrated by Jock in 1922, at Alpachiri, and demonstrates once more his artistic ability.

If Jock was still suffering from the effects of war, his time in this area of indescribable beauty must have provided him with a peaceful escape. From the desolate and scarred landscape of the Somme he had been transferred into a 'Garden of Eden'. The dense forest of laurel and walnut trees gradually made way for the Yungas (warm valley) jungle with dank reeds hanging from the branches of the trees. Towards 2,000 metres, there were outbreaks of meadow, carpeted with mountain flora, where rare bird-life thrived. Even higher, the Andean condor soared and ocelot, red deer and puma roamed freely. Such is the beauty and importance of this area as a natural habitat, combined with the need to protect the Incan ruins, whose importance was not realised until recently, that in 1995 the Argentine government decreed that it would become a national park: Parque Nacional Campo de los Alisos.

Section of illustration from *A Tale of Inca Times*
by Jock Campbell, 1922

For the next eight years Jock lived, as far as is known, on his own at his mountain *puesto*, at other accommodation in the area of Alpachiri or at his club when he visited Buenos Aires. Dorothy never again travelled to Argentina. Furthermore, the split in their relationship, the UK Philippis' provision of financial support and Dorothy's humiliation caused by Jock's affairs, had led Ernst's eldest son, Alexander, to warn his extended family that if any of them should ever visit Jock in South America they would be shot.

Dorothy had been part of the Philippi family for many years, always spending Christmas with them at Crawley Court. She had been fond of her Uncle Ernst, whom she described as a 'man of great probity and generosity',[8] qualities that she admired deeply and which, at times, were lacking in Jock. When she returned to the UK, her marriage in tatters, a property at Crawley was offered to her as a home. Ernst's children, George, Alexander and Dora, had looked kindly upon Dorothy and also funded her children's education. Since Ernst's death, George had continued to develop the estate and its houses. As well as the main house at Crawley, the Dower House had been restored and there was also Pond Cottage, in which Jock and Dorothy had stayed in 1917. Dora, who was of a similar age to Dorothy but had never married, had remained on the estate and they may have become companions. The Dower House was given as Patrick's home address when he started at Blundell's in September 1920 and Crawley Court was given as the address when Michael entered the school a year later.

Dorothy's parents had moved from Buxton to London in 1913, not long after Jock and Dorothy returned to Argentina, and young Michael remained in their care in the UK. In 1915 Margery, Dorothy's sister, had married Alfred Beal and in the early 1920s Madeleine, the other sister, was having an affair with William Dugdale Jackson, who was separated from his wife. Jackson's marriage had been a mistake and as he was a man of independent means he possessed the financial clout to proceed with a costly divorce. Madeleine, aged thirty, married William, aged twenty-six, eight days after the decree absolute was granted.

Madeleine had been living with her parents at 93 Philbeach Gardens, and after years of looking after her infant nephew Michael and caring for her, now-ageing, parents she was able to start a life of her own. Despite their age, Dorothy's parents remained on their own at Philbeach Gardens until, in 1924, tragedy struck. John Philips was then eighty-three and had remained active, both physically and intellectually, but one day in March he was struck by a horse-drawn baker's van when crossing the road. He suffered a compound fracture of his left leg and whilst being treated at a nursing home septicaemia set in; on 21 March he lost consciousness and passed away.

In the autumn of 1924, Patrick moved from Blundell's to Highgate School, North London, and two years later Michael entered Aldenham School in Hertfordshire. With her children now settled into senior boarding schools, in or close to London, and with her sisters married, Dorothy now provided support to her mother Alice, eventually moving in with her in Edith Road, West Kensington. It is not known exactly when, but at some time Dorothy converted to Catholicism. She had decided upon this faith whilst teaching at a convent at Neuilly-sur-Seine, on the outskirts of Paris. At the age of eighteen, Dorothy's linguist father sent her to Paris to improve her French. Dorothy had written to her parents asking for their permission for her to convert to Catholicism, but it was not forthcoming. Not only was she young and impressionable, her parents believed that it would reduce her chances of a good marriage. This was ironic given the circumstances in which she now found herself, but the conversion meant that she would not consider a divorce, despite the fact that her life with Jock had now passed.

After the death of her mother in 1936, Dorothy moved out of London to Lostwithiel, Cornwall, where her sister was living with her bank-manager husband, Alfred Beal. With little financial security Dorothy rented part of a little damp cottage in Albert Terrace, where she remained throughout the war. Dorothy remained in Lostwithiel until 1955, when her now-successful son Patrick rescued her and found rooms for her in Barkstone Gardens, Kensington, at his expense. Here, the pious Dorothy, following her conversion to Catholicism, was able to regularly attend the Brompton Oratory, a famous Catholic church in Kensington. Dorothy had been brought up in a strict Victorian household and in later life she came across as severe and straight-laced and totally at odds with the cultural changes taking place in London in the 1960s. In 1966, becoming frail, Dorothy went to live with an old friend, Jessie Carlisle, in Greet, a hamlet just north of Winchcombe, Gloucestershire. Jessie O'Brien, as she was when Dorothy first met her, was the daughter of an *estancia* owner whose land was some seventy miles away from Los Dos Hermanos. Dorothy died in 1967 and the wake, at Jessie's home, was attended by her son Patrick, and her grandson Alexander.

Jock's life in Alpachiri, whilst idyllic at times, was probably a commercial failure. Although his business revolved around timber, the economy of Tucumán province, and more particularly Concepción and Alpachiri, depended on sugar production. Between 1920 and 1925 the international price of sugar fell by 80 per cent, and this, combined with the lowering of production costs in Tucumán, meant that Argentina was flooded with cheap sugar. The Argentine sugar industry started to collapse irreversibly in 1924, and with it the local economy in Jock's area.[9]

Jock's mortgage was due to be repaid in June 1927 and it is not known whether this was achieved or if he had to forfeit his land and property. He was in Buenos Aires at the end of 1926, but again it is not known if this was a short visit or a permanent move. Jock certainly visited Buenos Aires whilst living in Alpachiri, and on one of his trips he met an Englishwoman, Gladys Pemberton, who had emigrated to Argentina in 1920.

Gladys was a rather plain, thirty-two-year-old spinster when she arrived in Argentina, one of eight children of a government clerk, Wriothesley Russell Henry Pemberton. Of the eight siblings, only three had survived by the time she left England: her; Beatrice, her married sister; and Ethel, who was looking after their father and who would visit Gladys in Argentina after his death in 1923. During 1927 Gladys told Jock that she was pregnant with his child and subsequently gave birth, on 20 September 1927, to Maria Isabel Pemberton Campbell.

The birth was nine months after the Christmas and New Year festivities in Buenos Aires, which included an ex-servicemen's ball on New Year's Eve. Had Jock developed a long-term association with Gladys during the 1920s, after Dorothy had left, or was this a one-night stand during the holiday season? Whatever the relationship, Jock registered the birth and perjured himself to protect Gladys and Isabel, implying in the birth registry that he was married to Gladys, as Isabel is named as their legitimate daughter. He also used the same Anglicised name for his father that he had used when marrying Dorothy: Henry Campbell.

In Germany Jock's brother, Richard, was carving out a successful career at IG Farben, which would become infamous and Nazi-run during WWII. IG Farben was the German equivalent of ICI in the UK, an almost government-controlled corporation, formed by the amalgamation of a number of companies. In the case of IG Farben, this was a merger of the founding companies of the German, if not the world, chemical industry, namely BASF, Bayer and Hoechst, which included Cassella and Agfa. Richard had come up through the ranks of Cassella and then with IG Farben he had become a deputy director.

Unrest and economic decline were causing instability in Germany and Hitler's National Socialist German Workers' Party was on the rise, helped by funding from IG Farben. However, Richard had developed cancer of the larynx and was forced to resign from the company; he died weeks later in January 1930. Richard was a wealthy man. He had been careful with his inheritance, whilst Jock had been profligate, and as a result he owned an apartment in Frankfurt and a twelve-acre estate in the country, fifteen miles north of the town. The land was bought in 1922, and would have been partly financed from the proceeds of the sale of Los Dos Hermanos, which Richard had received in 1920.

Richard Philippi

To provide for his children, Richard had set up a trust under the control of Professor Erwin Selck, a colleague. Selck and Richard had progressed together in Cassella, and Selck had become a director and the senior lawyer at IG Farben. Richard could not have known, in 1930, how both Selck and IG Farben would change during the next fifteen years. IG Farben became inextricably linked with the Nazi machine and Selck would become a Nazi officer, funding his own SS cavalry troop. After the war, most of the management of IG Farben were tried for war crimes at Nuremberg, the worst of which was associated with the manufacture and supply of Zyklon B, a cyanide-based pesticide used in the holocaust gas chambers. Selck died in 1946 and avoided the trial. Richard's granddaughter recalls how her mother hated Selck, but was not free of his guardianship until 1938, by which time Selck's sympathies were known.

Shocked at the news of Richard's untimely death, concerned for his sister-in-law and her children, possibly realising his own mortality, and without significant assets or income, Jock decided to end his relationship with Argentina. Gladys, together with their daughter Isabel, had already returned to the UK in 1929. Jock bade farewell to Alpachiri, made his way to Buenos Aires and, keeping up appearances, enjoyed a few days at his club before taking his first-class berth on board the *Highland Chieftain*, bound for London. Arriving in England in September 1930 must have been bittersweet for Jock, as he would have been faced with many complicated relationships to avoid or overcome: an estranged wife; two sons, who had all but disowned him; a mistress and child; a grieving family in Germany; the furious UK Philippis and a disappointed, but loving, mother. He would also have heard of the tragic death of his aunt Adela's twenty-eight-year-old son, Douglas Culross, in 1929. Douglas, who was still living with his parents in Harrogate and who had travelled to the Arctic with his step-uncle Francis ten years previously, died from an infection caused by polluted water he had drunk on a rugby field.

After the war Francis had resumed his polar exploits and as well as the trip with Douglas he continued to visit the Arctic every summer, as he had done since 1906. In 1926 he was again in Tromsø, from where he sailed to the Arctic on the *Hobby*, as advisor to the American millionaire explorer Louise Arner Boyd. In 1927 he was off again with the hunter Charles Peel, and by now he had shot 416 polar bears and captured others for European zoos, a pastime that would not be so accepted today. However, 'A more generous, truthful, unselfish, kind-hearted man than de Gisbert does not exist' was how Peel described him. Such was his reputation he also said that 'Everyone in the Arctic Circle loves the jolly fellow'.[10]

Initially, Jock would have stayed at his club, the Junior Naval and Military, in Piccadilly, although later that year Jock joined his sister-in-law in Switzerland. Margrit suffered from TB and each year spent October to December at the Waldsanitorium in Davos, where the clean air and available treatment gave her some respite. Other family members joined her when they were able, and Elsa Pfafferott, Margrit's sister-in-law, an artist and somewhat bohemian character, was present during Jock's visit. In December 1931, after her annual visit to Davos, Margrit took her daughter Edina, who was almost eighteen, to London, probably for the debutante season. The Philippis were well connected, both in Germany and the UK, and Edina and her sister, Margarethe, would later marry into German aristocracy. During their time in London, both Margrit and Edina were introduced to Gladys and her young daughter, Isabel. They must have made a favourable impression, as, in spite of the circumstances of Isabel's birth, it later became known that not only did Jock's German family accept them, but that they continued to correspond for several years. Although the relationship between Jock and his sons was difficult at this time, Michael also met Edina, whom he apparently adored.

It is unlikely, but if Jock had moved in with Gladys after his return to the UK, it did not last long. He is more likely to have been an itinerant, moving between his club, family in Germany, and hopefully Northumberland, where his mother lived, before she died in December 1931. By 1935 Jock was living in a boarding house in Linden Gardens, Notting Hill, all but destitute. Driven by the need for work and income, Jock applied to the Empire Officer's Guild, a charity set up by Earl Haig's wife in 1928 to assist officers who had served in the Great War to obtain employment. It is not known if he was successful in his endeavour but he remained at Linden Gardens until 1937. During this time and in this area of London, family hearsay suggests that there was yet another scandal involving Jock. Nothing is known of the incident, but Jock moved on to Ray Court, Shrewsbury Road, a mile north of Linden Gardens, and into an even lower-cost area of Paddington.

As the downward spiral continued, Jock's health may have suffered and the long-lasting impact of war may have been troubling him or affecting his personality. With no family support, which is hardly surprising, and little or no income, Jock suffered some sort of trauma whilst in the

Camberwell area in April 1938. He was rushed to Kings College Hospital, but instead of being treated there was immediately transferred to the Maudsley Hospital next door, a psychiatric hospital which during WWI specialised in neurasthenia. Jock must have been involved in an incident or had a breakdown and been taken to the nearest hospital and then, willingly or forcefully, transferred to a more suitable place for treatment. He was admitted to the Maudsley on 19 April and was not released, remaining an inpatient for almost a month.[11] Then, whilst under treatment or observation, Jock suffered a heart attack and on 13 May he died. The original reason for Jock being taken to Kings College Hospital could not have been heart-related, as if that had been evident he would not have been transferred. An autopsy revealed that the primary causes of Jock's death were myocardial degeneration, coronary thrombosis and arteriosclerosis, which led to his heart attack.

Jock was not alone when he died; Irene Ashworth, who worked and resided at 1 Vicarage Gate, was present and was the informant when his death was registered. Vicarage Gate was home to a residential care centre of the Distressed Gentlefolk's Aid Association, a charity established in 1897 for elderly gentlefolk in reduced circumstances. This resonates with the condition in which Jock found himself and so it is conceivable that he had contact with this organisation. However, Irene, at the time a fifty-year-old spinster, was not a stranger to Jock, as they had met twenty-seven years earlier in Hartington.

Florence Irene Ashworth, known as Irene to avoid confusion with her mother, also Florence, was the youngest daughter of the Revd Ashworth, the incumbent at St Giles' Church, Hartington, when Jock and Dorothy rented Pool

Hall in 1911. Was Irene the subject of the affair which Dorothy alluded to in her letters at that time and the catalyst for the move away from Hartington in 1912? Knowing Jock's eye for the ladies and his natural charm, it is a possibility that cannot be dismissed at a time when Dorothy was pregnant with Michael. How did Jock reacquaint himself with Irene? Had he maintained contact with her over the intervening years? Was Irene the subject of the family rumour of another indiscretion after his return to London? The answers to these questions may never be known. Jock's final resting place is also unknown. The antipathy towards Jock, by his immediate family and possibly Gladys, at the end of his life was such that there are no family records of a burial or funeral. It may well have been left to Irene Ashworth to lay Jock to rest.

Jock was enigmatic to the end. Having pushed his family away because of his behaviour, he died in the presence of a caring lady from his past. The complex man who was gifted in so many ways also had his faults which, towards the end of his life, may have been exacerbated by failing mental health. Together, these issues eventually destroyed his familial relationships, as well as himself. Living relatives can only recall him being described as the black sheep of the family or a rake. However, the early affectionate cartoons of his beloved Doly-Booboo and his illustrated story for niece Edina reflect another side of Jock, which should not be forgotten, nor should the possible long-term effects of his neurasthenia.

6

Like Father, Like Son – WWII

If your descent is from heroic sires, show in
your life a remnant of their fires.

Nicolas Boileau

Adolf Hitler became chancellor of Germany in 1933, but the position of president, and its incumbent, Paul von Hindenburg, was a block to his megalomania. This was resolved in August 1934, when President von Hindenburg died and the German cabinet enacted a law abolishing the position of president. Hitler became both Führer and Reichskanzler (Leader and Chancellor) and as a result was the Supreme Commander of the German Armed Forces. On becoming chancellor in 1933, Hitler ordered the army generals to increase the size of the army from 100,000 to 300,000 men. The former size was the limit imposed on Germany under the Treaty of Versailles after WWI, in which conscription was also forbidden. In 1935 Hitler was sufficiently confident to publicly declare that Germany was not keeping to the conditions of the Treaty, and furthermore that conscription would be implemented with a view to increasing the army to 580,000 men.

Against this backdrop, as tension rose across Europe, the families of the three John Campbells in Argentina, Germany and the UK were facing a decade of turmoil and change from which they would never entirely recover. In Argentina, John Argentine's children, Roderick, Tony and Joan, were living at and tending their inherited *estancia* at Carlos Casares; John Burnet's children were working in commerce in Buenos Aires. In Germany, Jock's nephew Herbert was enjoying a young bachelor life in Frankfurt and his niece Edina was courting Hubertus Graf von Korff gen. Schmising, whom she would marry in 1939. Finally, in the UK, Patrick, Jock's eldest son, had graduated and embarked on a career with Horlicks, whilst Michael was working at British Homes Stores.

As with Jock, university had not beckoned for his son Michael, who instead had joined BHS, a new venture in London established by a group of American entrepreneurs who wished to emulate the success of the Woolworths chain. Michael had started at the bottom of the company as a porter, straight from Aldenham School, and worked his way up and into management. From 1935 Michael rose rapidly within BHS, being posted from store to store across the country, as well as a spell at their Head Office in Brixton. By 1939 he had risen to become the Supervisor, General Stores, in Chester, where he lived with his wife. However, Michael's personal life during the previous four years had been complicated and, as is later discovered, all was not as it seemed.

By the time of Jock's death in 1938 his estranged wife, Dorothy, and their two sons, Patrick and Michael, who had given up on their philandering father, had little or no contact with their German relatives. They certainly had little to do with Jock's paramour Gladys, or his illegitimate daughter, Isabel. However, Jock's widowed sister-in-law, Margrit, and her daughter Edina, who had visited England from Germany in the early 1930s and met both Gladys and Isabel, had remained in contact by letter. After Edina's wedding in 1939, Margrit sent a photograph to the twelve-year-old Isabel with a note on its reverse. The note was dated 1 July 1939 and read, 'Dear Isabel, I am sure you would like to have a photo of Edina in her wedding gown! Thanks very much for your letter – I hope to see you in September. Much love from Aunt Margrit.'[1]

The German conscription system, reintroduced by Hitler in 1935, involved taking in all males as they reached twenty-one, which would have included Margrit's son, Herbert, in February 1938. However, it is more likely that he volunteered to join the army as an officer cadet, enabling him to choose his preferred unit, the historic and crack Goslar Jäger battalion. Volunteering also gave young men the opportunity to complete their officer training over two years, and then in peacetime return to civilian life as a reservist.

Herbert had been educated at a boarding school in Schondorf am Ammersee, twenty-seven miles west of Munich, but did not continue his education at university, unlike his academic father. He was a flirtatious, happy-go-lucky character who, in the lead up to the war, had yet to decide on a career. Herbert was a strapping young man with a passion for sport and a first-rate skier, all excellent credentials for joining the Goslars, a battalion whose history dates back to a Hanoverian regiment which

fought as part of the British king's German Legion under
Wellington at Waterloo. His choice of the Goslars would
have been influenced by his maternal grandfather, who had
served with them. In addition, his mother had grown up
in Goslar, which remained the home of his grandparents.

Herbert Philippi

During 1939 Herbert completed his training with the
Goslars, otherwise known as the 3rd Battalion of the 17th
Infantry Regiment, which in turn was part of the German
31st Infantry Division, formed in 1936 from soldiers within
the Brunswick region, of which Goslar was part. On 1
September the 31st Infantry Division, as part of Germany's
Tenth Army XVI Motorised Corps, invaded Poland. The
Goslars were part of this invasion force and, for all intents,
Herbert's war had started. Britain immediately declared
war on Germany and the note above from Margrit would

for many years end contact between the German Philippis and the UK-based Philippis/Campbells.

When war broke out, Michael was still living in Chester, and several months later his wife gave birth to a son, Donald. Conscription in the UK had started in 1939 for those aged between twenty and twenty-three, moving up the age bands as required until forty-one, the maximum age for conscription under the 1939 Military Training Act. In July 1940 Michael was called up as one of the twenty-eight-year olds. By then he was General Manager of the Northern Division of BHS, a position that warranted exclusion from military service had he wished to make that choice.

Michael's older brother, Patrick, was out of the UK at the beginning of the war, having been posted overseas by Horlicks. In 1942 he enlisted and underwent basic training with the RAF in India and was granted the temporary rank of flight lieutenant. Patrick spent the war with Air Command South East Asia in an administrative capacity. Following the war, Patrick resumed his career with Horlicks, and after spells developing the business in India, China and Australia, rose to become its managing director. As a young man Patrick never married and had no children, but in 1988, in the twilight of his life, he married Irene Howells, his long-time partner. Patrick died in 1991 and Irene followed in 1993. They are buried together in the Philippi graveyard at Crawley Court.

As was the case in WWI, when fate pitted Jock against his brother, Richard, their sons Michael and Herbert now found themselves on opposing sides in WWII. The Philippi family dynamics had changed in the intervening years so the concerns were neither as widespread nor as acute as felt by Ernst and Magda at Crawley Court. Ernst's children, who had fought for the British in WWI, were alive, but had nothing to do with the German side of the family and also had no children of an age to participate in WWII. Jock's children, Patrick and Michael, were not partial to their German relatives either. Things were different in Germany, especially for Edina, who must have suffered the most. She had a soft spot for her cousin Michael in the UK; had just married Hubertus, who was destined for the German Army; her brother Herbert was already fighting in Poland and her godmother, although born in Hamburg, was British and living in Lancashire.

The link between the British and German families was not entirely severed by the war: Edina's godmother, Alice Edina Sharp, who had no children of her own, left her entire estate to Margrit and Edina when she died in 1946. Edina died in 2000, but her reluctance during her life to talk to her children about WWII, her UK relatives or her German ancestors meant that her surviving daughter was totally unprepared for the approach I made to her in 2011.

After the invasion of Poland and action in France, Herbert moved to the Eastern Front for the invasion of Russia. Operation 'Barbarossa', as it was called, was the largest invasion in the history of warfare, utilising over four million troops, but would become overshadowed by tales of atrocities, the staggering death toll and the ultimate failure of the operation. News of atrocities were being picked up at Bletchley Park, which was staffed by members of MI6 and the Government Code and Cypher School. They were tasked with, and were successful in, breaking the codes of encrypted German wartime messages.

Herbert's 31st Infantry Division was now part of Panzergroup 2, led by Lieutenant General Heinz Guderian, who reported to Army Group Centre. Guderian had previously been commander of Herbert's Goslar Jäger battalion, and by the end of the war would rise to become Chief of the General Staff of the German Army. On 22 June 1941 the invasion of Russia began and Herbert was in the forefront as part of Guderian's *blitzkrieg* tactic of moving swiftly and annihilating all that was before it. Army Group Centre entered Russia, via Poland, with the job of taking Bialystok then Minsk, in modern-day Belarus, followed by Smolensk and then Moscow. Remarkably, Panzer Group 2 reached Smolensk, more than four hundred miles into Russia, by 14 July and after three days of heavy hand-to-hand fighting they took the city.

The Jäger battalion had been part of the rapid push into Russia, but by August they were withdrawn from the front line to recuperate as other units continued towards Moscow. During this time Herbert wrote home and talked of future family holidays and of better times ahead, without the cruelties and hardships of war. By October Herbert was back at the front preparing for an attack on Tula, only 120 miles south-east of Moscow. The wet autumn had made motorised transport almost impossible and progress was slow, added to which troop supplies were not getting through. This position worsened when, at the beginning of November, winter arrived with a vengeance. The soldiers sometimes went without bread for over a week and their winter uniforms had not yet arrived. As the temperatures plummeted to between -15 and -30 degrees Celsius the situation became intolerable. The soldiers were suffering from frostbite and were lacking the strength and possibly the inclination to fight the well-fed and warmly clad Russians.

Guderian was concerned and on 4 December, wanting to gauge the situation first-hand, he visited his old, and Herbert's current, Jäger battalion to talk to the officers. He needed to ascertain if the battalion had the strength to attack again, which they confirmed. Guderian remained concerned that the remainder of his Panzer Army were not so inclined, but the meeting convinced him to try once more to take Tula. In the event, the exhausted soldiers failed and a couple of days later Guderian heard that the German Third and Fourth Armies, despite reaching within twenty miles of the Kremlin, had been unable to push on to their ultimate prize. It was the turning point of the war on the Eastern Front.

Guderian withdrew his troops to a defensive position behind the River Plava, and for the whole of 1942 and the spring of 1943 Herbert was bogged down in defensive positions near Juchnow and Viasma. By the summer of 1943, Herbert's Jäger battalion was on a continual retreat, moving south-west away from Moscow. Finally, in June 1944, the 31st Infantry Division was almost completely wiped out near Minsk.

What exactly happened to Herbert is a mystery. Apparently the little of the division that survived was split, with some soldiers remaining with the Army Group Centre, which eventually became trapped in Latvia. However, Herbert somehow resurfaced in Estonia, as Oberleutnant Philippi, a reserve officer of the Marine-Artillerie-Abteilung (MA). It appears that between the summers of 1942 and 1944, Herbert was stood down from the army and automatically became a reserve officer. But the MA was under the command of the German Navy and Herbert was now an officer in 31 Schiffstammabteilung, a naval probation unit. MA units could also be land-based in order to provide coastal defence, which is what Herbert was doing. It is likely that, as the German Army North made their desperate attempt to flee from Estonia by sea, Herbert's artillery unit was tasked with providing protection against the Russian Army sweeping across from Narva. Bravely holding a position at Konju, a mile inland from the Baltic Sea and on the road from Narva to Tallin, Herbert and his men were eventually overrun.

Herbert was killed in action on 20 September 1944. When Margrit was eventually notified of the details of her son's death she was also informed that he had been posthumously granted the German Gold Cross, an award issued for repeated acts of bravery or repeated outstanding achievements in combat.

The onset of the second global conflict, only twenty-one years after the end of the first, stirred patriotic emotions in the children of the John Campbells living in Argentina. As their fathers before them, they had no legal obligation to opt for military service. However, the pull of the 'Old Country' remained strong and all of their children of service age would become involved in the war effort.

John Burnet's sons, John and Edward, returned to the UK and joined the British Army; and the children of the gallant John Argentine all made their contribution in very different ways. Joan had moved to London in May 1937, taken an apartment in St Mary Abbots Court, Kensington, and at some time after 1939 joined the Women's Auxiliary Air Force (WAAF) as an ambulance driver. Roderick, who had set his sights on a commission in the prestigious 1st Battalion Black Watch (Royal Highland Regiment), arrived at Liverpool on 12 July 1940 aboard the aptly named

Highland Patriot, and by September was undergoing basic training as a private in Perth.

Roderick, 2nd Lt R. Campbell, Black Watch

Tony, who, as his father, had been a Cambridge rugby Blue remained at the *estancia* as he was recovering from an operation to correct the long-term physical effects of polio, which he had contracted in 1931. He had a gregarious and sports-loving personality, but had been wheelchair-bound since the onset of his polio: a situation his mother, Myra, found difficult. In the coldness alluded to earlier, she almost shunned her son. Tony's answer was to take himself off with a couple of friends to live a louche life in Tahiti, following in the footsteps of Gaugin. On his way home, he apparently stopped off and spent time in Hollywood, where he was able to win over the actresses with his easy charm.

Towards the end of the 1930s Tony decided to take action to alleviate his condition, which, because of his time in a wheelchair, had developed into a curvature of the back. He visited Franklin D. Roosevelt's Warm Springs facility in Georgia, USA, where he underwent a horrendous pioneering operation. After the procedure Tony was placed in a full-body cast, in a bent-backwards position, for nine months. The result was near miraculous and, after convalescing at home, Tony was able to walk with crutches, and never needed the wheelchair again. However, he was desperate to do his bit during the war, but had to find the what and the where.

**Tony Campbell. Photograph of sketch
by Augustus John, London, 1944**

By November 1940 Roderick had completed his basic military training in the ranks at the Black Watch Infantry Training Centre in Perth. The first hurdle had been overcome and early in 1941 Roderick made his way to the 164th Officer Cadet Training Unit (OCTU) at Barmouth, in North Wales, to commence his officer training. After his first month, Roderick's ambition to become an infantry platoon commander in the Black Watch suffered a setback. His company commander had reported that Roderick 'appears nervous about expressing his opinions', 'appears to lack drive' and finally that 'he would do himself more justice in an administrative sphere'.[2] After his second month, little had changed and he was considered too old to grasp tactics and map reading.

It was true that he was on the older side, thirty-four at the time, and although being passed as A1 fit the army hierarchy was unaware that Roderick had been born prematurely, resulting in deafness in one ear. In addition, Roderick did not possess the academic and sporting prowess of his father and brother, and had not progressed to university from Fettes. These disadvantages, whilst hindering his officer training, made his commitment more remarkable.

On 19 March 1941, before finishing his training, Roderick had to complete army form E.562, setting out his regimental preferences once commissioned. In first place was the Black Watch (Royal Highland Regiment), against which he stated that he was purely Scottish by descent. This echoes the pride of the Argentine Scots, who, as previously mentioned, always maintained they were visitors to Argentina even though, in Roderick's case, both his parents and himself were born in Argentina.

A few weeks later, his spell at Barmouth ended and his Company Commander held to his view that the position of infantry platoon commander was not the right one for Roderick. On 6 April 1941 the commanding officer of the 164th OCTU agreed with the previous comments and finished with, 'His experience and ability to handle men makes him very suitable for a commission in the Pioneer Corps.'[3] Roderick must have been crestfallen upon reading and signing his report on 8 April 1941, as he was no longer destined for the Black Watch.

A month later, having accepted his fate, temporarily at least, 2nd Lt R. Campbell was transferred to No. 3 Pioneer Corps Training Centre, at Ilfracombe. After three months' training Roderick was assigned to the Mediterranean Expeditionary Force and shipped to Lobatsi Camp in Bechuanaland, a British Crown Colony, now Botswana. Here, the British recruited and trained local men for the war effort. In January 1942 the Company moved out of Lobatsi Camp, after the men had been issued with razors in order to shave their pubic hair to help eradicate an infestation of lice. This was a blessing, as the Company had three months of travel ahead of them and would be in close proximity to each other during this time.

Roderick's final destination was Rayak, forty miles inland from Beirut, where, instead of leading an infantry platoon of the Black Watch, he was one of four officers managing a black work-gang laying railway track. In addition, conditions were poor at Rayak, where mosquitoes were breeding and creating a malaria risk. It is not surprising that Roderick had, since joining the Pioneer Corps in the UK, continued to agitate for a transfer to the Black Watch. However, such agitation must have fallen on deaf ears as on 25 May Roderick travelled to Beirut to be interviewed for a transfer to the Indian Army. He was unsuccessful and remained at Rayak until October, during which time more railway track was laid, cabling removed and smallpox and malaria avoided.

The following month Roderick's company was split. He became Officer Commanding of one section and was promoted to lieutenant. A few days later he received even better news when 47 Group HQ informed him that the commanding officer of the 1st Battalion Black Watch was prepared to accept him into the regiment. Roderick's desire and push for the transfer must have been relentless; his CO, Major Pickford, remarked, with a hint of annoyance, 'This officer came from Argentina on purpose to join that regiment and has worked unceasingly to obtain his transfer there.'[4] After several months training with the Black Watch, both in the UK and at their training camp in Algeria, Roderick was finally appointed infantry platoon commander of B Company of the 1st Battalion; his military ambition was now fulfilled.

Roderick's men had completed a successful campaign at the Battle of El Alamein in Egypt, followed by a push across the north of Libya to a triumphant entry into Tripoli. They had regrouped and trained in preparation for their next campaign, the Allied invasion of Sicily. The Allied powers decided in 1943 that as a precursor to an assault on France in early 1944, they should attempt to capture Italy, as an Italian surrender would provide a major propaganda coup and allow the Allied naval forces to dominate the Mediterranean. In January 1943 a top-secret deception was planned to lead Hitler into believing that the Allies would attack Sardinia and Greece, rather than Sicily. It involved planting a dead body in the sea, to which was attached a briefcase containing fake documents about the planned attacks. The documents, when found, were passed to German Intelligence, which resulted in troops being deployed away from Sicily. Operation Mincemeat, as it was called, was later made into a 1957 film called *The Man That Never Was*.

The Black Watch sailed out of Valletta harbour on 9 July, in very rough seas, and the Allied forces attacked Sicily on 10 July 1943. On landing, Roderick's regiment encountered little opposition with no casualties, other than a soldier who had died from seasickness en route. The regiment pushed on, moving north across a fertile plain, and by 14 July were camped near the tree-lined road that led to Buccheri, where they received orders to attack two targets in the vicinity. Allied artillery opened up to cover the infantry, but at 11 p.m. the artillery fire for the second objective fell instead on Roderick's battalion, with the friendly fire killing one officer and wounding thirty-five men. Apart from this error the operation was a success and during the next two days the battalion moved further north.

Until now, Roderick had not witnessed much hostility from the retreating German Army, but at Gerbini things changed, as this strategic area included road junctions, a railway station, an aerodrome and barracks, making it important for the Axis forces to defend. The fighting was fierce and although the Germans did not succeed in halting the advancing Allied forces the 1st Battalion suffered greatly in the Battle of Gerbini. It had all of its tanks knocked out and there were nine killed and thirty-one wounded. The battalion was withdrawn from the area, retreating to an anti-tank ditch, and on 25 July a memorial service was held for those lost in the battle. On the same day, Roderick was admitted to hospital. The battalion war records do not give a reason, but one might assume that he had been one of those injured in the past day's fighting.

Within days the Allies had taken Sicily and entered the Italian mainland. However, the Black Watch were held back, remaining in Sicily to relax and recuperate before moving back to the UK at the end of October 1943. The battalion was billeted at Berkhamsted and for five months they languished and trained, during which time Roderick was able to visit his brother and sister in London. In April 1944 the battalion moved out to Southwold and within days a lockdown was ordered, censorship of all mail commenced and closed orders were instituted. Day and night river crossing training exercises began, and on 8 May a table of personnel for Operation Overlord, the code name for the invasion of Normandy and the D-day landings, was issued.

On 23 May Roderick learnt that his injury, incurred at Gerbini, was to rule him out of the operation. He was not the only officer or soldier to be transferred from the battalion that week, with only the fittest remaining to take part in what would become a vital part of the beginning of the end of the war. Roderick was not to see front-line action again and spent the rest of the war in staff positions in the UK.

Roderick returned to Argentina a few months before the end of WWII and in October 1945 resigned his commission due to disability. He was granted the honorary rank of lieutenant and ran his *estancia* until his death. After his wartime experiences he resolved never to go anywhere where he could not have a bath every day. In September 1969 he attended the second rugby test match between Argentina and his homeland of Scotland. Surprisingly, Argentina had won the first test and the second and final test was very close; eventually Scotland won by three points. It must have been a bit too close for Roderick, who suffered a heart attack and died during the match, at the Gimnasia y Esgrima stadium.

The drive of Roderick's brother, Tony, to join the war effort had borne fruit, and in July 1942 he travelled to the UK and moved in with his sister in Kensington. Tony had sought the help of his friend Bill Bentinck (Victor Frederick William Cavendish-Bentinck, who became the 9th Duke of Portland in 1980) to find a suitable job in London. Bill was chairman of the Joint Intelligence Committee (JIC) and managed to get Tony a desk job at the Foreign Office.

By this time Bletchley Park was intercepting German coded messages and it was apparent that atrocities were occurring, initially on the Eastern Front. Churchill and the War Cabinet were being made aware of this, but were unable to use the information, as this would have provided the Germans with the knowledge that their messages were being intercepted and decrypted, a fact that was kept secret throughout the war. Nevertheless, the JIC was asked to catalogue the instances of atrocities; it set up a small unit comprising of a lawyer, Roger Allen (later Sir Roger Allen, Ambassador to Greece, Iraq and Turkey), 'assisted by another Foreign Office official a Mr Campbell' (Tony).[5] The unit received information from Bletchley, wrote it up and regularly presented it to the JIC.

Another task set for Tony during his spell at the Foreign Office was to review the evidence for the Argentine claim to the Falkland Islands. He concluded, as have others since, that on the four bases for territorial claims the Argentines did not have a case. Throughout this time Tony worked from an upper floor at the Foreign Office and caused great consternation, as he was the only person in the building unable to get to an air-raid shelter in the event of an attack. Although he was no longer in a wheelchair, descending stairs on crutches required the support of others.

Tony married his English wife, Mary Sant, early in 1943 and moved into an apartment on the King's Road, London. In July 1944 they returned to Argentina, where Tony continued to manage his *estancia*. He died in 1985 and his son continues to run the same El Jabali estate established by Tony's father, John Argentine Campbell, in 1904.

Tony's sister, Joan, remained in London after the end of the war, although both of her brothers had returned home. In September 1946, either as a holiday or a permanent return, Joan decided to travel back to Argentina. Her chosen method of transport was by air rather than the longer sea voyage her brothers had taken, possibly influenced by her time in the WAAF. Joan travelled on an Avro 685 York, operated by British South American Airways, and its route was to take her from London to Buenos Aires via Lisbon, Bathurst (the Gambia), Natal, Rio de Janeiro and Montevideo. The plane, *Star Leader*, landed at Bathurst in the early hours of the morning of 7 September and took on a new crew. At 4 a.m. they took off for Natal. The weather was fair, visibility good and there was little wind.

Shortly after take-off the aircraft struck some trees, crashed into the bush, rolled over and burst into flames. Joan, the nineteen other passengers and four crew were all killed. It was the captain's first Avro York flight on a scheduled service and it was also the first take-off he had made in a York, loaded to more than 69,000 lbs. The cause was considered to be loss of control by the captain, probably due to his mishandling of the controls.

By July 1943 the war had raged for almost four years: Dunkirk, the Battle of Britain, the fall of France, Belgium and the Netherlands, and the battles of Tobruk and El Alamein had all passed. In the meantime Michael Campbell had willingly left his senior role at BHS, joined the ranks of the Scots Guards, been identified as officer material, passed out at Sandhurst, and practised his skills as an officer in rural Fife. He had been commissioned into the same 1st Battalion Black Watch as the unrelated Roderick Campbell, but had yet to see active service. His family were settled in a farmhouse in Easter Friarton, Fife, and Michael had been able to spend time with them whilst based in the area.

In August, Michael received his posting, wrote his army will and was shipped to North Africa. But by the time he arrived that campaign was over and the Italian campaign had begun, with the Allies having already taken Sicily and reached the toe of Italy. Front-line action was only days away for Michael, as he was to be attached to the 2/6 Queen's Regiment at Salerno as part of Operation Avalanche. This was the plan to attack Italy on the west coast, as the British 8th Army moved up from their success in the south of the country. However, Michael would miss the initial invasion as he was still making his way from Africa.

Operation Avalanche was planned for 9 September and by the night of 8 September the 5th Army had sailed across the Mediterranean from various ports and had massed offshore. An armada of forty-five ships, containing 100,000 British and 69,000 US troops, lay in wait.

That evening, news was broadcast over the ship's tannoys that Italy had surrendered. The troops, thinking the job had been done, were quickly told that the Germans, without the aid of the Italian army, would be fighting with even more determination to quell or delay any move by the Allied forces into and across Italy.

At dawn on 9 September Allied troops landed across a fifteen-mile stretch of the Italian coast, in and around Salerno. The 2/6 Queen's were amongst the first to land and faced fierce opposition. The regiment had already been under-strength when they landed, and casualties in the first three days at the beachhead had exacerbated the situation: on 12 September they reported a shortfall of 188 officers and men. Two days later, the Allied forces secured the beachhead at Salerno and the following day additional troops, including Michael, arrived to take the regiment back to its full complement of 700 men. The 2/6 Queen's moved inland and then turned north via San Severino, Castel San Giorgio, Siano and Sarno, bypassing Naples to the right.

By 15 October they had crossed the Volturno river and while Michael and 2/6 Queen's patrolled the road to Bellona, the 2/5 Queen's pushed on to Calvi Vecchia, where they encountered resistance. The 56th Infantry Division, of which 2/5 Queen's was part, decided to call in air support for a bombing raid on the village, which was planned for 11 a.m. on 18 October. As 2/5 Queen's moved up towards Calvi Vecchia that morning, the resistance had dissipated and they found themselves walking straight into the village unchallenged. Realising that the Germans had retreated, the bombing raid had to be called off or a hundred men of 2/5 Queen's and the remaining villagers would be in peril. However, the wireless failed and connection with the

US airbase was lost. At 10.30 a.m., with communications to the airbase still out, British 10th Corps Headquarters, who were in contact with the soldiers, released an American Army service pigeon with a message. The pigeon, GI Joe, flew the twenty miles to the airbase in a record twenty minutes and the message was received as the bombers were on the runway, preparing to take off; disaster was avoided. After the war GI Joe received the Dickin Medal for bravery.

Two days later Michael and his men passed through Calvi Vecchia, but once through they encountered heavy fighting, with many killed and wounded over the next three days. After a further six weeks of action, in difficult terrain and appalling cold and wet conditions, 2/6 Queen's were relieved by 46 Division. It was during this period of heavy fighting in difficult conditions that an administrative error at the front caused Dorothy to be mistakenly informed of her son's death in action. In fact, Michael had made it back south and across the Volturno with the rest of his regiment, to their billet at Falciano Selice. There on 23 December he was able to write to Padder, as Dorothy's children called her, to apologise for the distress and inform her that he was safe and well.

Michael had many of his father's traits: romantic, at ease with people, not suited to academia, a dreamer. However, he had proved he was an excellent manager at BHS and now the army recognised his leadership skills in the field and under fire. In January 1944 Michael was promoted to Officer Commanding, B Coy, 2/6 Queen's, with the acting rank of major. The push north continued, and Michael and his regiment were involved in heavy fighting for a month. They had crossed the River Garigliano and were heading towards Monte Cassino and Rome when, in mid-February, they were ordered to withdraw to Naples, re-equip and prepare to sail to Anzio further up the coast.

Despite Operation Avalanche having begun on 9 September, the position by mid-February 1944 was becoming fragile, as the Germans reinforced and prepared themselves for a series of counter-attacks in Italy. The enemy was holding their line in an arc running from the coast north of Anzio around to the south, in a radius of six to ten miles. In the middle of the month, the German forces were able to burst through the line in several places and fierce fighting broke out, resulting in a high casualty count on both sides. The allied forces prepared a counter-attack for 19 February and two task forces were formed, one of which was led by 169 Brigade, including Michael and the 2/6 Queen's.

The troops of 169 Brigade had embarked and were sailing towards Anzio on the evening of 18 February, but the next morning they came across survivors from HMS *Penelope*, which had sunk following a torpedo hit by a German U-boat. The survivors were brought on board and returned to Naples. This postponed Michael's arrival until 20 September and his regiment were further delayed at the harbour whilst remaining mines, dropped by enemy aircraft, were cleared. As 169 Brigade were no longer available, the counter attack had to be scaled back, using only one of the task forces. Finally, the brigade made it onto the beach and headed inland towards the left flank of the Allied forces. Despite the absence of 169 Brigade, the counter-attack had been a success. Many German soldiers had been captured and the death toll had been so great that an Allied prisoner of war would later recall that he saw piles of bodies behind German lines, which had to be shifted by bulldozer into mass graves. The Allies also suffered, with more than four thousand lost or wounded during the month, a tally which was not helped by the lack of respite on the beachhead.

In the days that followed, 2/6 Queen's was involved in such heavy fighting near the ravines feeding the River Moletta that A and C companies had to be merged. Reports then came in of an enemy-occupied house in Pontoni and the remaining platoons of B company, led by Michael, set off to investigate. They were followed, an hour later, by two more companies from the regiment, who arrived in time to witness the incredible action, which is reflected in the regiment's war diary.

> 24 Feb. 04.00.
> C and D Companies were enthralled spectators from a distance of 250yds. of Maj. Campbell and B Coy clearing the party of Bosch from their objective. It was difficult not to cheer and applaud what was such fantastic entertainment. B Coy took objective with small arms and hand to hand combat fighting, killing 5, capturing 12 with the loss of only one slightly wounded.[6]

On 15 June 1944 the Military Cross was awarded to Michael with immediate effect, for his action that evening. His commendation mentions Michael's 'personal bravery and complete disregard for his own safety'. It concluded, 'Throughout this action, Major Campbell displayed the utmost coolness and dash, and his personal example and leadership was entirely responsible for inflicting severe casualties on the enemy, as well as driving them from a key position.'[7]

Soon after this action, the battalion was withdrawn from the front line, exhausted. They were moved to Naples,

then to a safe billet, where they were issued with fresh
battle-dress before being shipped to the Dalmatian island of
Vis. Here, there were many cases of malaria and smallpox,
and on 3 May Michael suffered one of these fates and was
transferred to 92 General Hospital, where he would remain
for a number of days before moving to a convalescent
depot. His illness must not been too serious because at the
beginning of June Michael rejoined his regiment, which
was now re-supplying and taking on new troops in Egypt.
Some leave was taken during this time and Michael had a
few days in Cairo, whilst the rest of the month was spent
training in the desert, in intense heat.

Michael Campbell, Major R. M. Campbell MC, July 1944

The regiment was shipped back to Italy on 17 July, with further training continuing until the end of August, when Michael moved up towards the front line at Fossombrone, twenty miles inland, on the east coast of Italy, south of Rimini. On 31 August, 169 Brigade moved out to the hills north of San Giorgio and 2/6 Queen's were ordered to attack Monte Capella at first light. The fighting was heavy and casualties were incurred, but the regiment pressed on. The following day Michael's B Coy were ordered to attack a place west of Mondaino and, although successful, Michael was injured in the arm, but carried on. The German Army was desperate to hold the Gothic Line and fighting in the Apennines was intense for the whole of the month. The bloodiest battle was for the hill town of Gemmano, which lasted from 4 to 15 September, and which has been described as the 'Cassino of Northern Italy'.

Michael was heading in that direction, but 169 Brigade had been ordered to hold back in reserve until the Gothic Line had been broken. Instead, B Company skirted Gemmano, taking up a position near Croce, before succeeding in taking Passano, against much opposition, on 19 September. Towards the end of the month Michael moved north across the plains west of Rimini heading for Savignano, which stood on the Via Emilia, the path taken by Julius Caesar in 49BC on his way to take Rome. When Caesar, approaching from the north, reached Savignano he and his legion had to cross the single bridge over the River Rubicon, which signified the border of Italy, controlled by Rome. It is said that as he reached the bridge he tossed a die in order to decide whether or not to continue with an illegal march on Rome, giving rise to the saying 'crossing the Rubicon', meaning a point of no return. On 27 September, almost 2,000 years later, Michael's B Coy were ordered to take the very same heavily guarded bridge at Savignano.

Michael literally and metaphorically crossed the Rubicon, successfully leading his men to capture and cross the bridge, but then became surrounded by the enemy. In the ensuing skirmishes, as they tried to return to their own lines, they were caught in crossfire and almost all of B Coy were captured, wounded or killed. During the action Michael's right leg was hit by multiple machine-gun bullets, shattering his femur and grazing his back. He was able to describe what happened next in a letter to his mother, which he wrote from 83rd General Hospital at Riccione, just south of Rimini, on 3 October.[8] When Dorothy received the letter, so difficult was the pencil-written script to read that she marched off to Scotland Yard to enlist their help, where they apparently applied 'ultra red rays' to clarify the illegible paragraphs.

> Padder Dearest
>
> I am sorry to have to tell you I am once more wounded. Compound fracture of the right femur and a graze to the back from a German machine gun at 50 yards range, 8–10 bullets. I fear it will be three months before I can get up again and several weeks of orthopaedic treatment.
>
> I had one of the most unpleasant jobs to do.
>
> … most of my party were wounded or killed and I was made a prisoner.
>
> They treated me as well as they could – had no iodine and were short of water and food owing to our road shelling. They talked to me in German and gave me wine and water. They all asked how long the war was going to last: five years too long. They had had no hot food for days. I was being taken behind their lines but there was no transport thank God!

They came to me one morning [probably 30 September] and said they were going back and their officers insisted on shaking me by the hand, telling me the ambulance would be along in about four hours. The house I was in had the windows blown in and I spent the next day [probably 1 October] in agony unable to move.

Later the house was knocked down by our tanks. Add to this, heavy mortars and 25lb shelling all round. I should think it was pretty good second hell. I had two other wounded in the same house, one who could just walk and the other completely immobile not even being able to crawl for shelter from the flying glass. I just lay on an old doormat with a blanket over me with a sack of seed for a pillow. A whole day went by and no-one came.

I sent the walking case back to get help. But nothing happened and he did not return. The following day [probably 2 October] I heard Italian spoken and yelled for some water. A youth came in and I told him the trouble and he went to fetch some British stretcher bearers. I have never been so glad to see anyone. We could not move however for another six hours as the guns were shelling more in the area, being pulled out of it. The house again got hit. Eventually the stretcher bearers took me away, carrying me through shelled areas for nearly 2,000yds. I was then placed in a Thomas splint – agony having a leg stretched out and the bone grating especially as the wounds had not been attended to for three days.

I then felt better and all were very kind to me. I ended up at 83 General Hospital and was operated on within an hour of arrival. A new anaesthetic which had no after effects was used – excellent no hangover or sickness.

My leg is in plaster up to my hip and I am reasonably comfortable please thank God for me

for my deliverance. I don't know how long I shall
be here so address letters to the BW until I am
settled. Don't worry as I am in good hands and
comfortable I fear only a few of the company got
back and all were wounded I also got a burst across
my spine which only grazed it and a splinter which
tore my ear lobe will have plenty of time to write
and rest

all fondest love
Michael

As the Allied forces overran Savignano, the retreating
Germans blew up the two-thousand-year-old bridge and
moved north. Their retreat was so quick that they abandoned
equipment and vehicles, and left injured soldiers in random
buildings and field hospitals.

Having been operated on and stabilised at Riccione,
Michael was moved to 11th General Hospital, at Porto
Recanati, further south on the Italian coast. Michael was
in good spirits, but on the evening of 5 October there were
signs of heart failure and the nursing staff did not believe
he would survive. However, Michael rallied and at 8.15 the
following morning he cheerfully asked the Sister for a cup
of tea. He then closed his eyes and died.

Michael had shown a relentless spirit to survive and
was out of danger in terms of the broken femur; however,
he had succumbed to a fat embolism. Today, medical
professionals recognise that there is a distinct possibility
of such emboli occurring between five and seven days after
a major trauma or breakage of a long bone, and prophylactic
treatment is given.

Major R. M. Campbell MC had fought bravely as the
Allied forces swept north through Italy and is buried at

the Ancona War Cemetery. Oberleutnant M. A. d. Res. H. Philippi DKIG, just as bravely, provided rearguard action against the advancing Russian troops, during the German evacuation of Estonia but his body was never recovered. Lieutenant R. Campbell, despite his partial deafness, fulfilled his ambition to fight with the Black Watch. The Campbells and Philippis had indeed demonstrated that they had a remnant of the fires which their fathers had exhibited in WWI. However, war had, once more, extracted its price.

7

Heir-Hunting

M y discovery of Gladys Pemberton in the 1929 UK Incoming Passenger List was the jump-start for the necessary detailed research of Isabel Campbell's maternal family. By the spring of 2011 I had established that Gladys was born in 1888, the seventh of eight children, to Wriothesley Pemberton and his wife, Cresceat Allen. Only one of Gladys's siblings, Beatrice, had married, but there hadn't been any children from that union. As there was no issue from any of the other siblings, some of whom had died prematurely, any beneficiaries to Isabel's estate would have to come from her father's family.

I eliminated John Argentine Campbell as Isabel's father after I discovered his death in action in 1917. Then, in April 2011, having made no further progress to establish which of the other two John Campbells might be the father,

I contacted a genealogist in Buenos Aires. I wanted to establish the possibility, with so few details, of tracing Isabel's Argentine birth record. A month later an email from Argentina signalled success. Receiving Isabel's birth certificate enabled me, by chance, to establish in my own mind who her father was.

Amongst many of the documents I had collected relating to John Campbells with a link to Argentina was a page from the 1911 UK Census. It featured a household in Derbyshire which included an Argentine groom, Elias Ferreyra, and was signed by the head of the house, John Campbell. To my astonishment the census signature matched that of Juan Campbell on Isabel's birth certificate. It was unmistakeable and another chance occurrence; a finder's delight.

John Campbell's signature on Isabel's Argentine birth certificate (top) and on 1911 UK Census

Armed with the name of John Campbell's wife from the census, I was able to trace their wedding and order a copy certificate. The name of John Campbell's father in the marriage document (Henry Campbell) and Isabel's birth certificate (Enrique Campbell) matched. Another confirmatory revelation. I couldn't believe my luck. Surely professional heir-hunters must have reached the same conclusion. What other barriers could lie ahead? It had taken over a year to satisfy myself that I had my man, but I remained unable to confirm his place or date of birth or find any record of his parentage, which would be required if I was ever to make a claim on the estate.

I continued my internet desk research and discovered birth records for John Campbell's children born in the UK, Patrick and Michael. This, in turn, led me to a website forum containing a photograph of Michael. Unfortunately, it was a restricted site requiring permission to access and view the attachments. I emailed the forum host and quickly received a reply informing me that she was merely an unrelated conduit for the owner of the images. For days we tiptoed around the reasons for my request, as she acted as a go-between. I had realised, in the nick of time, that secrecy was important, because it had become apparent from other web postings that I was not the only detective on the quest for Isabel's heirs.

Under UK intestacy law Isabel's next of kin, given that she had no children or full-blood siblings, would be any half-blood siblings or their issue. As I had identified that my John Campbell had two children, two half-blood siblings of Isabel, I now needed to find any of their living children, which would pave the way for a claim. Realising that I might only be one generation away from Isabel's heirs changed my mindset. I was no longer an amateur genealogist, trying to find why others had failed to solve the case, but now an heir-hunter, closing in on potential family members who had a right to the estate.

The change in mindset altered everything. I understood how professional heir-hunters operated and wanted to emulate their process. For me it would be a challenge within a challenge. I wanted to see it through to the end, find living heirs, obtain their agreement to make a claim, possibly persuade them to agree to a finder's commission, and even assist or manage the administration of the estate, in the event of a successful claim. Giving up hard-gained information, especially within a public forum, was no longer an option, as it could have advantaged the professional competition.

Late one evening in May, I received a telephone call. It was the owner of the forum photograph, and after swapping some information that only he and I could know, I established that he was Michael's son, Donald, and therefore an heir to the estate. Shaking with excitement, I steeled myself to raise the subject of the estate of the illegitimate daughter of his grandfather. He was not surprised. As a teenager he had spent hours listening to Dorothy's story, whilst staying with her and his Uncle Patrick in London. He knew of Jock's past intrigues and described him as a rake.

Unfortunately, at the end of the conversation I was left with the distinct impression that he did not want me to pursue a claim on his behalf. Later, I formed the opinion that this was due either to a fear that any public revelations might tarnish the name of his war-hero father, or that other skeletons may remain to be found in the closet.

More time passed as I tried to assure Donald, via emails to the forum host, that I was genuine: I did not have his email address or telephone number, and without his compliance I could not make a claim on his behalf. However, the earlier telephone discussion with him had not been entirely unhelpful. Donald had led me to believe that Jock had been born in Germany, and that after leaving Germany he had changed his name.

This tied in with the name given for him, Jock Otto Campbell, on Michael's Commonwealth War Graves Certificate (CWGC), which I had accessed earlier, and which had confused me at the time. It was the first instance of the names Jock and Otto which I had come across. He had obviously been known as Jock, but was this because it was assumed he was Scottish or because his initials were JOC? As for Otto, I had not considered that his parents could have been German, but with Donald's input it now made sense. By the end of June, without Donald's support to make a claim and without the details of Jock's birth, I was almost ready to admit defeat.

Believing that Jock had possibly changed his name, I decided to search the online National Archive catalogue, but entering John Otto Campbell or Jock Otto Campbell produced no results. Then, as I had done so many times before when searching the internet for clues, I started to enter other combinations. Otto Campbell produced an immediate response, referencing the 1902 naturalisation papers of Otto Campbell Philippi, a German. I had a hunch that this was also Jock and that the file would contain the evidence I needed to bring some finality to what had become a fixation over the previous eighteen months.

It was a familiar walk from Kew Gardens station yet, as I neared the end of Ruskin Avenue, and the monolithic building housing the National Archives came into view, my expectations were higher than usual. I was early and the reading room had yet to open, so I made my way to the café and sat patiently amongst an anonymous group of researchers, academics, historians and students, all waiting to commence their research. At nine-thirty I moved upstairs and collected a sturdy buff box which housed my pre-ordered documents in a folder marked 'Not to be opened before 2002.'

Upon opening the musty folder, I saw that a letter, dated 1917, had been inserted into the front of the file, which had previously been closed in 1902. It referred to a John Campbell, formerly known as Otto Campbell Philippi, and was a request for permission to sail back to Argentina at a time of war. Not only did I have Jock's birth name, but also his naturalisation papers, which remained intact and provided his date of birth, his parents' names and a host of other information to help me tease out the details of Jock's early life.

One final piece of information eluded me: the date and place of Jock's death. It should have been a simple internet search through the online index of deaths, but nothing was forthcoming. Had he died outside of the UK? Could a variant of his name have been registered at death? In the end the answer was simple, although the search had been difficult, and the problem was down to a shortcoming in technology. Had I visited the General Record Office and searched the hard copy index it is likely that I would have discovered the information immediately. However, the online database that I searched uses OCR (optical character recognition) to extract data from an image of the hard copy index, and in this case John Campbell had been read as Joan Campbell. Another trap for the unwary genealogist.

Everything required by Bona Vacantia to unlock the estate was now in place, but I still needed a living heir to agree to the submission of a claim, and I remained hopeful of persuading Michael's son, in order to complete my heir-hunting challenge. However, as more months passed, my overtures to Donald continued to prove unsuccessful, and with any claim on Isabel's estate looking unlikely I continued to research Jock's family.

With more online investigation I discovered and contacted a member of the Philippi family in Germany who, as a hobby, was writing up the family history. This in turn led me to the name of Jock's brother's granddaughter, Verena Auffermann. She is the daughter of Edina, who had met Isabel in London in the 1930s. Born Verena Elisabeth Gräfin von Korff gen. Schmising, she is descended from one of the oldest noble families in Germany: the Westfalian Catholic branch of the Korff family, whose line can be traced back to the twelfth century. I was anxious to contact her, and after finding an email address for someone with the same surname I trotted out a request for any knowledge of Verena. It was her nephew who responded, and within days I was having a fantastic email dialogue with Verena in Berlin. If there hadn't been any issue from Jock's children, Verena would have been next in line to claim the estate. She was a first cousin once removed from Isabel and a second cousin of Donald.

Contact with Verena opened the door to Jock's German ancestry and over the months that followed we continually surprised each other with information. She with letters, photographs and images of the book Jock had written for her mother in 1922, and me with history of her family, including her Jewish roots, of which she was unaware. I also managed to contact Dorothy's side of the family, tracing and visiting the grandson of her brother, Commander Philips, who was also able to share information and images with me.

I was frustrated, yet resigned, at getting so near and yet so far with the claim when, in early November 2011, the postman delivered a weighty A4 envelope. I had completely forgotten that months before I had ordered Michael's Army Service Personnel Record, which now lay before me. Over the past few months, I had assumed that Donald's mother was married to Michael, as was stated on his birth certificate and Michael's CWGC. But I was about to discover that genealogical research can play tricks on those who make too many assumptions, even from official documents. Within the records was Michael's enlistment paper, which named his wife as a different woman and included a son of a different name, together with a note saying, 'Separated from wife by mutual consent.'[1] The search was back on; my original heir, Donald, had a half-brother, Alexander.

I now had to backtrack my research to 1935, when the young Michael was moving around the country with BHS. His charm, like that of his father, had worked on a stunning seventeen-year-old girl, but this relationship resulted in an unexpected pregnancy. Michael, however, did the honourable thing and married the young woman, an option not open to Jock in 1927. Several months later they had a baby boy, Alexander, and after a spell with BHS in Margate the family moved on to London, where they set up home in an apartment in Cromer Villas Road, Putney.

Michael was now working at the BHS store in Putney, where he remained for a couple of years, other than during trips to cover at other locations, or to work at Head Office in Brixton. His relationship with his wife deteriorated, perhaps because his lust had not changed into love, and this resulted in at least one break up and reconciliation. His wife had yet to reach twenty and was about to discover that Michael had another amour in London. She was a beautiful, strong-minded woman, three years older than Michael and had been living with her father in Brixton, until his death in July 1937. Their house was a short walk from the BHS Head Office and it is possible that she also worked for BHS.

The discovery of this liaison in 1938 was the final straw for Michael's wife and their relationship ended acrimoniously, despite the comments to the contrary in Michael's army records. Michael, needing some space, then scuttled off for a holiday in Paris and the south of France. On his return he took up with his new partner, and by 1939 they were living together in Chester as man and wife.

I now had two heirs to Isabel's estate, Donald, who did not wish to make a claim and who had been born out of wedlock to Michael's partner, and Alexander, the legitimate child of Michael and his lawful wife, whose whereabouts was unknown. Trying to trace Alexander required more investigative work, but by discovering various relatives of Michael's wife I eventually tracked down a cousin, who was able to confirm that he was alive and agreed to get a message to him with my contact details. A week later I received an email from Alexander and a four-month discussion began.

Alexander, like Donald, needed to be convinced that my approach was not a scam and he wanted to build some trust between us. He was also unsure about making a claim, did not want to become involved in detailed discussions with third parties and was concerned about raking over the past. I was able to assure him that I would handle all contact with Bona Vacantia and his half-brother, and that in the event of a successful claim I also agreed to administer the estate on his behalf, through a power of attorney. This was sufficient to persuade Alexander to allow me to submit the necessary papers to the Treasury Solicitor in London.

In March 2012 I collated some documents and made an initial approach to the Bona Vacantia department. My journey to solve the case and to discover an eligible heir, who was willing to allow me to make a claim on their behalf, was complete. If the claim was successful, each heir would receive 50 per cent of the net estate, irrespective of whether or not they agreed to make the claim. As the wheels of the government office handling the claim slowly turned, my mind moved at last to Isabel. I knew nothing about her: she was just a name picked from a long list.

8

Isabel

The life of the dead is placed in the memory of the living.

Marcus Tullius Cicero

The internet had provided many of the leads needed to unravel the details of Isabel's relatives, but I drew a blank with regards to Isabel herself. Instead I resorted to a more traditional method and cold-called people in and around Petworth who may have been able to shed some light on Isabel's life. These calls led me initially to a neighbour, from whom I heard, for the first time, the circumstances of Isabel's death. However, it was a breakthrough that was to lead me to some of Isabel's friends, godchildren and finally to relatives of Isabel's husband.

Although surprised at being tracked down and initially willing to talk, some of her closest friends eventually withdrew their support, wishing to keep their thoughts and memories of Isabel to themselves. This may have been partly driven by their negative thoughts of living heirs who had no knowledge of Isabel, and who did not wish to learn more about Isabel directly through them, inheriting her estate. Her friends believed Isabel to be a very special person with great qualities, including a charming and a gregarious nature, which chimed with my understanding of her father. It is understandable that these dear friends did not want to revisit the grief of Isabel's untimely departure, but remain with the warm recollections of their good times together. I gathered what titbits came my way and, with additional deep research via the internet and at the British Library, I was able to piece together a picture, albeit incomplete, of Isabel's life and character.

Isabel was born on 23 September 1927 at Sante Fe 899, Buenos Aires, the offices of Dr John Halahan, an Irish-born obstetrician and GP who was also physician to the prestigious Hospital de Clinicas. Her birth was registered by Jock and witnessed by Gladys Haddock, a forty-two-year-old widow whose husband had died after a fall from his horse on his ranch in 1916. Gladys was living in Buenos Aires with Henry Baker, the second witness, and was now a secretary, possibly working at the British Legation with Isabel's mother, also Gladys.

Isabel and her mother remained in Argentina after her birth, but it is not clear if Jock played any part in their lives. Two years later Gladys may have given up any hope of a long-term relationship with Jock in the Argentine and sailed back to England with Isabel, on the *Deseado*, and arrived at Liverpool on 20 July 1929. From there they made their way to London, where they stayed with Gladys's widowed sister, Beatrice, at her apartment in Sandringham Court, Maida Vale.

A fifty-year-old Jock followed Gladys back to England in September the following year, his brother Richard having died in Germany in the previous January. Jock had some contact with Gladys and Isabel on his return, and in 1931 he introduced Richard's widow, Margrit, and daughter Edina to them both. However, it is unlikely that he ever lived with them. During this time Jock's sons also met Margrit and Edina, but whether or not they met their half-sister is unknown.

Gladys, at some point, moved on to an apartment of her own, in Richmond, with sister Beatrice taking another property in the vicinity, on hand to provide support. Isabel grew up only seeing her errant father occasionally before he died when she was ten. But, however difficult her upbringing, Isabel was ably provided for and educated by her mother. She was writing to her Aunt Margrit in Germany before she was ten, and by the time she was eighteen had developed into a confident and attractive young woman. Towards the end of WWII Isabel was training to be a nurse at St Bartholomew's Hospital, an early indication of her caring and selfless nature.

A few years later, as she reached the age of majority, Isabel contemplated the process of British naturalisation, as she had been born in Argentina. Her naturalisation file, unlike that of her father and her great-uncle Ernst, no longer exists, but may have provided interesting additional information, other than her address and occupation. By the time her naturalisation was completed in 1951, Isabel was working in another vocational role, as a School Assistant, giving further credence to the generous nature referred to by her friends and family.

Isabel, with the surname Campbell and a Scottish grandmother, developed a strong affinity with Scotland. Some of Isabel's husband's relatives believe that she sought roots that were missing due to the lack of contact with her father, and regular trips were taken to the Highlands. On one such visit in the 1950s she met, at a *céilidh*, her future husband, Ian.

Isabel Campbell, c. 1945

Gerald Ian Greig was the only son of Captain Gerald Andrew Greig and Vera Francis. According to one source, Ian had apparently suffered from polio when he was about twelve and, although he recovered, it left him a little weak and unbalanced at times. His mother, in an apparently strained second marriage, was totally devoted to her only son, such that when he attended Stowe School she moved into a cottage on the school estate to be near him. One might doubt that this could have helped his time at Stowe, between 1939 and 1941, where he did not distinguish himself or proceed to university.

His army father was also not impressed when he failed to get a commission in the army, instead joining the ranks of the Royal Hussars towards the end of WWII. This differs from his embellished obituary in the *Scotland Herald* and the *Times*, which have him leaving school, being commissioned into the cavalry at the onset of the war and unwittingly capturing German tanks in the Netherlands. In fact, Trooper G. I. Greig remained with the 15/19 Hussars after the war and was posted to Palestine, apparently rising to the rank of corporal, before leaving in 1949.

When Ian's father died, in 1950, Ian inherited a life tenancy of a family trust, providing him with an income for life. Ian's grandfather Robert Gillespie Greig had been a partner in Wright & Greig, a distillery owner and spirit merchant, and the trust had emanated from that business. During the 1950s Ian dabbled in journalism, before becoming involved in politics and meeting Isabel.

Later in life Isabel and Ian would be seen as inseparable and were described to me as being 'like two peas in a pod', but when they met, it may have been a case of opposites attract. Ian was slightly bookish, shy and somewhat scruffy, with dark unkempt hair. Isabel on the other hand was slim, attractive, confident and generous in spirit; more Jock than Gladys. Apparently they were made for each other: Isabel lent some extroversion to Ian, and Ian gave Isabel a financially stable partner and the Scottish link she craved. But Ian's shyness probably led to his inability to propose to Isabel.

Time has dimmed the memories of those recounting the details of their engagement, but it was certainly not as a result of a direct proposal from Ian. Either Isabel herself proposed, or as another family member suggests, it was at a time when Isabel and Ian were together with his mother who, despite her doting relationship with her son, saw an obvious pairing and engineered the proposal herself. The former would highlight Isabel's strength of character and assertiveness and the latter a mother's frustration at her son's procrastination.

By 1959, when they were married at the Holy Trinity Church, Brompton, Ian was working as a political agent within the Conservative Party. Up until then Isabel had been living with her mother in Richmond and Ian was residing in an apartment on Brompton Square. The witnesses at their wedding were Gladys Campbell (sic), her mother, who had in the past changed her name from Pemberton, and Ronald Haughton Watson MC, Ian's cousin and also a Conservative Party member. Once married the couple moved to an apartment in Thurloe Square, possibly owned by Ian's family trust, and Isabel began assisting Ian with his research and becoming immersed in his politics.

I have been told that the couple worked, lived and travelled together, though Ian's life is far more documented because of his political associations. Ian and his friends had strong, radical, right-wing views which, following Harold MacMillan's famous 'winds of change' speech, in Cape Town in 1960, led them to form the ultra-right Conservative Monday Club. MacMillan was the Conservative prime minister in the UK at that time and a promoter of African de-colonisation, which to some right-wing Tories was not the preferred political strategy. The Monday Club was set up as a ginger group in protest and as a defendant of South Africa and white Rhodesia. Ian remained the Monday Club membership secretary until 1969.

At the same time Ian, who had become interested in the study of terrorism during his time in Palestine, was also focussing on communist subversion. This was a subject upon which he would become an acknowledged expert, and according to his dubious *Times* obituary would have him labelled as an enemy of the state by *Pravda*. The West had progressed to the height of the cold war and Ian had started to write anti-communist propaganda for research organisations, funded by the US and UK intelligence agencies. In 1962, the MP John Biggs-Davison had joined the Monday Club, and Isabel, Ian and the Biggs-Davison family remained close throughout their political and personal lives. Biggs-Davison was also inextricably linked to counter subversion organisations.

The iconic 1960s in London witnessed seismic cultural and political changes, including the downfall of the Conservative government, but Isabel and Ian's life together was probably more cerebral than pop. They were children of the 1950s rather than the '60s and much of their social life revolved around Ian's political network and family. Isabel organised Ian's life, always accompanying him on his travels, maintaining his diary, taking photographs and arranging soirees at their home. Isabel's mother, who had remained in Richmond, joined them at Christmas, other feast days and Greig family gatherings. She is recalled as a quiet lady, diminutive, hunched and very different from her, altogether louder, soul of the party, daughter.

By 1964 the couple were living in a larger apartment in Ennismore Gardens, close to Harrods, where I was told Isabel had a penchant for shopping. Here Isabel played a most accomplished and genial hostess to an assortment of politicos and members of the British and overseas intelligence communities. Gladys, in her late seventies and ailing, moved in with her daughter in 1966 and passed away in 1967. Isabel reported the death and, interestingly, entered Jock's occupation as Turf Accountant, providing a clue that she, or at least Gladys, had knowledge of what her father had supposedly been doing on his return to the UK in 1931.

When Jock died in 1939, Irene Ashworth registered his death and gave his occupation as Commission Agent, which, at a time when off-course betting was illegal, meant a person who took bets and passed them to a bookmaker on the racecourse, in return for a commission. A Turf Accountant on the other hand could also mean someone who accepted bets on the racecourse and took the financial risk. Whether Jock went as far as taking that risk is not known, but it can be assumed that his interest in horses and horseracing was rekindled on his return to the UK. This interest could have been inspired at the turn of the century by his friend Russell Monro, who was a successful point-to-point rider and trainer.

Despite being rather shy and not having shown academic prowess at school, Ian was quietly becoming an expert in communism and anti-communist propaganda. In 1968 Ian cut his publishing teeth on *Assault on the West*, with a forward by Sir Alec Douglas-Home, and by the end of the decade had become chair of the Monday Club's Subversion Committee.

Isabel had, by 1973, become the organiser of the Zanzibar Society, where Biggs-Davison was vice-chairman, and was also working for the South Africa Society, a right-wing pro-apartheid group.[1] Obviously her politics were aligned with those of her husband and the membership and committees of these societies would overlap with the work Ian was doing. In addition, both Isabel and Ian were in close association with the South Vietnamese government, whose embassy was also in Ennismore Gardens. There Isabel organised *Focus Vietnam*, which supported the South Vietnamese effort in the UK, whilst Ian worked on pro-South Vietnamese propaganda.[2]

The Monday Club and Isabel and Ian's involvement with the South Vietnamese government was featured in a sarcastic and negative article in a 1973 edition of the satirical and anti-establishment paper *Private Eye*. The article concluded, 'Monday Club members, when not concealing their connections with neo-Nazis and the South Vietnamese Government, have found time to support other euphemistically named groups such as the Foreign Affairs Circle, the Democratic Alliance and the Anglo-Rhodesia Society.'[3] In other words the same shadowy and government-funded organisations with which Ian would spend most of his working life.

Right-wing politics aside, Isabel became concerned, as the Vietnamese war progressed towards its conclusion, with the plight of its war orphans. She became involved in efforts to help them and for her work in this area the South Vietnamese government, prior to its fall in 1975, decorated Isabel.

Ian continued to be closely associated with numerous right-wing associations during the 1970s, which were usually propaganda outlets, posing as a research institutes, funded by various UK and international intelligence organisations, as alluded to in *Private Eye*. These included the Institute for the Study of Conflict (ISC), whose council was peppered with senior security chiefs, and the Foreign Affairs Research Institute (FARI), financed by the South African government. In 1979 Ian became the Senior

Executive at the ISC, whilst maintaining his position as Deputy Director of FARI.[4]

By the 1980s subversion was less of an issue and there was an increased focus on anti-terrorism. The Guildford and Birmingham pub bombings, perpetrated by the IRA, had occurred in 1974; FARI's own Airey Neave was assassinated in 1979 and the Hyde Park and Harrods' bombings followed in 1982 and 1983. Isabel and Ian had now moved out of London and were settled in Petworth and Ian's input became more advisory, as he wound down his ISC and FARI activities. However, he remained for a time, together with his now knighted friend, Sir John Biggs-Davison, on the board of another institute, the Research Foundation for the Study of Terrorism, set up by Professor Wilkinson, who had been advising Margaret Thatcher on the subject.[5] In 1986, prompted by the Harrods' bombing a few years before, Isabel and Ian together with the Biggs-Davison family set up a charity, The Combined Emergency Services Fund, to help those affected by terrorist activities.

Living in Petworth brought Isabel and Ian physically closer to Ian's family, who lived near Amberley, but Isabel missed being near the action in London and in particular Harrods. However much Isabel may have hankered after life back in the city, it was not something she would dwell on, as she was never seen in a mood, never angry and apparently never had a bad word for anyone. Isabel's life was always in the present or the future.

By the end of the decade, Isabel and Ian had been closely associated with quasi-political organisations for more than twenty-five years. Isabel had worked with a number of organisations and charities, but had also continually supported Ian in his endeavours. Their lives had revolved around politics and had brought them into regular contact with many famous names on the right wing of the Conservative Party, as well as heads of the intelligence community and the right-wing UK press. Isabel, at the same time, never lost sight or contact with friends and family, in particular her godchildren.

When Ian became ill in the 1990s, Isabel was always at his side and when the struggle was lost, so was Isabel. For forty years they had lived, loved and worked together and had rarely been apart. Now was the time for friends and family to rally, to keep her company and to plan ahead. Ian had written a will in 1976, leaving his estate to Isabel. They were not wealthy, their main asset being the house at Petworth, but at least there was no complication in Ian's estate passing to his wife. On the contrary, Isabel had never made a will and friends and family now urged her to do so.

Ian died in October 1995 and by Christmas that year the formalities of probate had not been completed. Talk of Isabel making a will had been postponed until the New Year, as had possible plans to visit Hamburg, to try to trace Jock's and therefore Isabel's relatives, something that might have given her purpose without Ian. When Isabel set off from Petworth, to spend Christmas with an old childhood friend in Bath, the weather was wet and mild. However, on Christmas Day the first item on the BBC news was that Scotland and northern England had suffered the worst snowstorms for forty years. After Christmas, the cold weather moved south and, with snow forecast, Isabel made plans to leave her friend and return to Petworth before the end of the month.

Isabel did not see in the New Year, but became a victim of the weather. Such had been Isabel's closeness to

Ian and her loss so painful that some have suggested that karma had now brought them together again. Others can see Isabel, reflecting on her life, raising her eyebrows and saying, with a mischievous twinkle in her eye, 'Rather fun, darling, don't you think?'

Without a will her estate eventually passed to the government and Maria Isabel Pemberton Greig's name sat for years amongst a list of thousands of others which remained unclaimed. Only a quirk of fate plucked her name from the list and triggered the search for her father, John Campbell.

Epilogue

There are no secrets that time does not reveal.

Jean Racine

The claim to Isabel's estate was finally accepted by the Treasury Solicitor in December 2012 and I began the process of probate. However, the administration of the estate presented yet another hurdle because Donald, who had not been a party to the claim but was an inheritor, remained suspicious of my overtures: I had not been the only heir-hunter to contact him. This situation was resolved once Donald finally realised that my actions were not part of a scam and I was able to distribute the estate to both of the heirs and close the estate accounts.

The search for John Campbell and the heirs legally entitled to Isabel's estate had tested my resolve, but also created in my mind's eye a picture of life in the cities and pampas of Argentina. However, would my interpretation match reality? To try to find the answer to this question I

embarked, in March 2014, on what felt like a pilgrimage
to Argentina. For almost a month I criss-crossed the
country searching for the *estancias* and townhouses of
the families I had come to know through research. The
guides, translators, archivists and family members whom
I met were so welcoming and helpful that, at times, my
discoveries were quite emotional.

I stayed at the de Rosas-built *estancia* once owned
by John Burnet Campbell's maternal grandfather, which
was instantly recognisable from the old photograph of
La Adela. The *estancia* is now called La Juanita and run
as a country lodging, and over afternoon tea I was able
to discuss the history of the house with its owner. Later
in the day she passed me her phone and I found myself
talking to a Dodds family member, a descendant of James
Dodds, who had owned La Adela with James Burnet.
Before dinner I wandered along the lake shore at the
rear of the house. The fox's tails were motionless in the
evening stillness and the crimson and gold of the sunset
was reflected on the lake amongst the reeds. A picture
unchanged with the passing of time.

In Monte Buey I was met by a local architect and
historian who, together with an interpreter, had agreed to
help me locate John Otto Campbell's *estancia*, Los Dos
Hermanos. We drove out of the town and along dusty dirt
tracks until we arrived at the now cultivated pampas, dense
with crops of maize and soya. Across a field the architect
pointed to a small copse hiding the ruins of Jock's house,
which had been inhabited until twenty years ago.

The structure of the barn remained standing and was
confirmed by photographs provided by Jock's grandson,
which I had taken with me. As we stood amongst the

vegetation-covered remains of the house, the architect became very excited as my additional images, together with the remaining walls of the *estancia* house, would enable him to digitally reconstruct the building. We also visited the beautifully renovated Los Algarrobos estate once owned by John Benitz, which Jock had visited in 1905. Finally, after making our way back into town I was introduced to the current owner of Jock's land, who showed me, in his garden, the wrought-iron patio gate which he had salvaged from Jock's house. It was a sad farewell as I took my leave of the architect, who presented me with a signed copy of his book of the history of Monte Buey, which included a reference to John Campbell.

I arrived in San Miguel de Tucumán hoping to meet a local archivist, but communication problems meant that we only had time for a brief meeting, over coffee, before I drove on to Alpachiri. It was here, sixty miles from San Miguel, that I believed Jock had settled after selling Los Dos Hermanos. I left the main road at Concepción and headed for Alpachiri, in the foothills of the Aconquija mountains. After eleven miles the tarmac road came to an end and I was back on a typical Argentine unpaved road, which after a short while led me to the trekking lodge I had booked for the night. The owner was fascinated by my plans to climb up into the national park the next day and insisted on guiding me, which turned out to be a blessing.

The following morning, in glorious sunlight, we drove a further ten miles away from Alpachiri, fording small streams and ascending up a boulder-strewn track, for which my small hire car was definitely not suited. Eventually we arrived at the entrance to Parque Nacional Campo de Los Alisos. The park ranger was initially unwilling for us to proceed because of the previous three days of heavy rainfall. However, he relented after a heated discussion with my guide, who I later discovered had told the ranger that I was a relative of a previous owner of the land and had travelled from the UK especially to visit the park. His persuasion worked and the ranger walked with us to the first mountain river. My plan was to climb up through the forest to a *puesto* in which Jock may have lived, but the swollen river seemed to have us beaten. My guide, the lodge owner, more confident than I was, walked across the stream in his boots and, leaving the park ranger behind, I followed.

For more than an hour and a half we climbed, wading up to our knees through swollen rivers along the way. The path was not particularly steep, but it was relentlessly uphill. The forest was dense either side of the path and the midday sun and earlier rainfall combined to produce an equatorial sauna. Eventually we reached a small meadow and a hut, but a sign showed that the *puesto* was another nine miles ahead, an impossibility for us in the allotted time, so we returned to the lodge. As I was about to leave Alpachiri, the archivist whom I had met briefly in San Miguel emailed me a 1920 mortgage document which he had unearthed. It described the exact area of the national park and proved that Jock had not only owned a property in the park, but the whole 25,000 acres, including the Inca ruins.

Back in Buenos Aires I was surprised to find, as I wandered through the historic *barrio* of San Telmo, that the apartment owned by John Burnet was still standing. The apartment block, built by the Swiss architect Christian Schindler in 1913, was Jack's home after his parents died. It is now described as one of San Telmo's most beautiful historic buildings and is often used for film shoots. The locals refer to the building as *El Edificio de los Ingleses* (The English Building), as it was originally designed to house British executives who came to Argentina to run the railway system at the turn of the century. It lies on the wide tree-lined Avenida Caseros and retains most of its original features, including its caged lift, marble steps and stained-glass windows. On the ground floor there is a restaurant, Club Social, which opened in 1920 and where Jack must have dined from time to time.

John Argentine's grandson, who had invited me to stay at Estancia El Jabali, picked me up in Buenos Aires and drove me the two hundred miles out to his farm. Before dinner we visited the amazing Estancia La Corona, whose current owner, the grandson of John Argentine's sister, Leila, gave me a detailed tour. We all returned for dinner to the house that John Argentine had built on his return to Argentina around 1905, where we talked about the history of the Robson–Campbell dynasty.

It was more than I could have reasonably expected when I had planned the trip; it enhanced the picture I had of Argentina in my mind's eye and was a magnificent and fitting end to my research.

The search for Isabel's beneficiaries was an extraordinary and unexpected adventure, during which secrets were revealed and the past illuminated. But it wasn't without its challenges; past wounds were opened and needed soothing; frustration from Isabel's friends, as her estate passed to those who did not know her, needed placating; surprise and sometimes suspicion by many who were contacted during the search needed assuaging. The families of three very different John Campbells were discovered and exposed, overlapping in time and space, each having their share of grief, joy, success and failure. All three have direct living descendants: grandchildren, great-grandchildren and great-great-grandchildren, whose lives, one hopes, are enhanced by the feats and memories of their patriotic and pioneering forebears, whose stories unfolded before me.

During my journey of discovery I was able to introduce Alexander to an unknown second cousin (Dorothy's great-nephew), who lived close to him in the UK, and also to Verena Auffermann (Jock's brother's granddaughter), another second cousin. As a result, Alexander and Verena struck up a dialogue. It was the first time the UK Campbell/Philippis and the German Philippis had communicated since July 1939, when Verena's grandmother had sent Isabel the photograph of her mother's wedding. Then in 2013, at Verena's invitation, Alexander travelled with his wife to Berlin. They were able to recount information about their families, share documents and enjoy each other's company. Alexander returned with a gift from Verena, colour facsimile copies of the book Jock had made for Verena's mother in 1922 and a sample card from Beit & Philippi, their great-grandfather's printing ink company.

Alexander's life had been marked by the loss of a father he never knew and who did not acknowledge him in his will. He also had, through necessity at the time, a transient childhood, living alternatively with his mother, grandparents, aunt and at boarding school.

His mother had remained in London after the breakdown of her marriage. She was young and realised that without any help from Michael she would need to earn a living to support Alexander. Her striking beauty and seamstress skills led her to a retail fashion shop in Regent

Street, where she modelled, and eventually managed the business. After the war she sent Alexander to boarding school for three years, funded from her hard work, and then embarked upon her own business, making exclusive wedding dresses. By the end of the 1950s she was remarried, and such was her success that she was able to open her own boutique on Bond Street.

Alexander became an industrial chemist as, interestingly, was his half-brother Donald, his Uncle Patrick, Richard, his great-uncle and Otto, his great-grandfather. It was not until he was almost forty that, after a discussion with his mother, he finally met his father's remaining family, Dorothy and Patrick, who have since died. But now, following my contact, Alexander had discovered additional family members on his father's side, of whose existence he had been unaware. It was an emotional yet gratifying experience for him.

Failure to find any living heirs would have left the estate in the UK Treasury coffers, as has happened to tens of thousands of other estates of those who have died intestate. But this search for John Campbell and Isabel's living heirs was never about money. It was, initially, a personal challenge, a quest for information that developed into an heir-hunting obsession. And the obsession eventually brought about something much more rewarding.

Notes

Chapter 1: Migration to Argentina

1. Anderson, *The Scottish Nation*, Vol. III, 355.

2. Dodds, *Records of the Scottish Settlers in the River Plate, and their Churches*, 23. <http://www.electricscotland.com/history/argentina/riverplatendx.htm>, accessed April 2014.

3. Ibid., 8–9.

4. Ibid.

5. 'Timeline of Edinburgh History', *Wikipedia*, <http://en.wikipedia.org /wiki/Timeline_of_Edinburgh_history>, accessed March 2014.

6. Grierson, 'The Voyage of the *Symmetry*' in Iain A. D. Stewart, ed., *From Caledonia to the Pampas: Two Accounts by Early Scottish Emigrants to the Argentine*, 44.

7. Grierson, 'The Voyage of the *Symmetry*'.

8. Dodds, *Records of the Scottish Settlers*, 38.

9. Ibid., 34–35, citing *Buenos Ayres British Packet*, 23 August 1828.

10. Rauch, *Conflict in the Southern Cone: The Argentine Military and the Boundary Dispute with Chile, 1870–1902*, 5.

11. Dodds, *Records of the Scottish Settlers*, 55.

12. Ibid., 56.

13. Ibid., 177.

14. Ibid., 193.

15. Hanon, *Diccionario de británicos en Buenos Aires : primera época*, 190.

16. Mulhall, *Handbook of the River Plate*, i, Section C, 126, <http://openlibrary.org/books/OL14051205M/Handbook_of_the_river_Plate>, accessed April 2014.

17. Fernández-Gómez, *Estancias y estancieros de barracas hasta el salado : la epopeya de los pioneros Británicos en el Campo Argentino*, Tomo B, 74.

18. Mulhall, *Handbook of the River Plate*, i, Section C, 18.

19. Sophie Campbell, 'On the Trail of the Galloway Gaucho', *The Daily Telegraph*, 8 May 2004, <http://www.telegraph.co.uk/travel/730249/On-the-trail-of-the-Galloway-gaucho.html>, accessed 8 August 2011.

20. George Campbell, 'Testament' (25 November 1869), Crown Copyright, National Records of Scotland, SC19/41/13, 853, <http://www.scotlandspeople.gov.uk>, accessed 9 August 2011.

21. Sophie Campbell, 'On the Trail of the Galloway Gaucho', *The Daily Telegraph*, 8 May 2004, <http://www.telegraph.co.uk/travel/730249/On-the-trail-of-the-Galloway-gaucho.html>, accessed 8 August 2011.

22. 'Argentina, censo nacional, 1869,' index and images, *FamilySearch*, <https://familysearch.org/pal:/MM9.1.1/M4WN-FTX >, accessed 27 May 2014. Patricio Campbell, Cuartel 05°, Monte, Buenos Aires, Argentina; citing Archivo General de la Nación, Buenos Aires; FHL microfilm 0668205.

23. George Campbell, 'Testament' (25 November 1869), Crown Copyright, National Records of Scotland, SC19/41/13, 849, <http://www.scotlandspeople.gov.uk>, accessed 9 August 2011.

24. Ibid., 854.

25. Robson, 'Faith Hard Tried: The Memoirs of Jane Robson' in Iain A. D. Stewart, ed., *From Caledonia to the Pampas: Two Accounts by Early Scottish Emigrants to the Argentine*.

26. 'Argentina, censo nacional, 1869,' index and images, *FamilySearch*, <https://familysearch.org/pal:/MM9.1.1/MWQ3-H47>, accessed 27 May 2014. Esperanza Blac, Gualeguay, Entre Ríos, Argentina; citing Archivo General de la Nación, Buenos Aires; FHL microfilm 683135.

Chapter 2: From the Land to the Landed

1. John Campbell, grandson of J.A. Campbell, email to John Daffurn (23 April 2012).

2. Ibid.

3. 'Walter Wren', *Wikipedia*, <http://en.wikipedia.org/wiki/Walter_Wren>, accessed 10 June 2012.

4. Lt.-Col. Norman Macleod, 'A History of the School 1870–1932' (1932), <www.fettes.co.uk/ofa/Hist270s.htm>, accessed 15 August 2011.

5. McClure, '1891–1896' in H. R. Pyatt, ed., *Fifty Years of Fettes: Memories of Old*, 151.

6. Stevenson, '1896–1902' in Pyatt, *Fifty Years of Fettes*, 154–5.

7. *Baily's Magazine of Sports and Pastimes*, 109 (London, 1918).

8. Graham-Yooll, *The Forgotten Colony: A History of the English-Speaking Communities in Argentina*, 48.

9. J. B. Campbell, 'Special Peace Number', *Revista Del Río de La Plata* (1919).

10. Sophie Campbell, 'A Flavour of Britain down Old Buenos Aires Way', *Financial Times* (23 April 2005), <http://www.ft.com/cms/s/0/7a917bd8-b393-11d9-ad2b- 00000e2511c8.html>, accessed 22 August 2013.

11. *Standard* (Buenos Aires, 12 March 1904).

12 Ibid. (16 March 1904).

13. Ibid. (5 April 1904).

14. Laffaye, 'Lewis Lacey: Master of the Game', in H. A. Laffaye, ed., *Profiles in Polo: The Players who Changed the Game*, 68.

15. Laffaye, *The Evolution of Polo*, 113.

16. Ibid., 114.

17. Ibid., 225.

18. 'The Past Hurlingham Season', *The Polo Monthly*, viii (1912), 19, <http://www.hpa-polo.co.uk/yearbooks/1912%20Sep%20 -%201913%20Feb.pdf>, accessed March 2014.

19. 'London Tournaments', *The Polo Monthly*, ix (1913), 406, <http://www.hpa-polo.co.uk/yearbooks/1913%20Mar%20-%20 1913% 20Aug.pdf>, accessed March 2014.

Chapter 3: The Making of Jock

1. Poliakov, *The History of Anti-Semitism: From Voltaire to Wagner*, 21.

2. Ibid.

3. Ibid.

4. R. Philippi, private chronicle of the Philippi family.

5. 'Advertisement', *Liverpool Mercury* (6 April 1875), <http://www. britishnewspaperarchive.co.uk >, accessed 15 April 2014.

6. 'Crown Court Proceedings', *Liverpool Mercury* (15 December 1875). <http://www.britishnewspaperarchive.co.uk>, accessed 15 April 2014.

7. R. Philippi, private chronicle of the Philippi family.

8. Ibid.

9. 'Beit & Philippi', *American Printer and Lithographer*, xix–xx (1895), 180, <http://books.google.co.uk >, snippet view accessed 15 April 2014.

10. 'Destructive Fire in Hamburg', *Glasgow Herald* (22 December 1892), <http://www.britishnewspaperarchive.co.uk>, accessed 29 November 2011.

11. 'Crew List for Vessel "*Maria*", 1869–1901', Gloucestershire Archives, 3080/60587.

12. Ibid.

13. 'British Merchant Navy Sea Schools', 16, <http://www.rakaia. co.uk/downloads/sea-schools/sea-schools.pdf>, accessed April 2014.

14. Ibid.

15. 'Midshipmen's Register Undated, Devitt and Moore', National Maritime Museum, DEM/18.

16. 'Voyage Book 1885–1917, Devitt and Moore', National Maritime Museum, DEM/28.

17. Lubbock, *The Colonial Clippers*, 233.

18. 'Voyage Book 1885–1917, Devitt and Moore', National Maritime Museum, DEM/28.

19. 'List of Officers and Cadets 1891–1908, Devitt and Moore', National Maritime Museum, DEM/17.

20. H. G. Adams, 'Log of the Ship Macquarie, 1898–1899', State Library of Victoria, Australia, MS 9519 MSB 469.

21. Ibid.

22. R. Philippi, private chronicle of the Philippi family.

23. 'Midshipmen's Register Undated, Devitt and Moore', National Maritime Museum, DEM/18.

24. 'Nationality and Naturalisation: Philippi, Otto Campbell, from Germany. Resident in London. Certificate 12579 issued 3 June 1902', The National Archives (TNA), HO44/649/B38135.

25. 'Long Service Papers. Lieutenant John Campbell. Royal Field Artillery', The National Archives (TNA), WO 339/2672.

26. Otto Campbell Philippi, 'Jewish Naturalisations', *Jewish Chronicle* (7 November 1902), 30, <http://www.british-jewry. org.uk/jcnaturalisations.php>, accessed March 2014.

27. 'Christmas Letters, The Postmaster-General's Experiment at Rochdale', *Manchester Courier* (27 December 1902), <http://www. britishnewspaperarchive.co.uk>, accessed 24 September 2014.

28. John Campbell, cable to Dorothy Philips (16 August 1903).

29. 'Announcements', *Manchester Courier* (19 December 1903), <http://www.britishnewspaperarchive.co.uk>, accessed 20 November 2011.

30. J. Benitz, 'Diary of John Benitz' (25 March 1905), <http:// www.benitz.com/BzJohn1861/BzJohnE1861_Diary1904. html#Year_1905>, accessed April 2014.

31. John Campbell, letter to Dorothy Campbell (17 May 1905).

32. Certified copy of birth certificate of Patrick Campbell, 24 December 1909, FD829409, Chorlton Register Office, Manchester, England.

33. John Campbell, letter to Dorothy Campbell (16 October 1913).

34. Dorothy Campbell, letter to John Campbell (4 November 1912).

35. Burn Murdoch, *Modern Whaling and Bear Hunting*, 221.

36. Otto Ernst Philippi, letter to John Campbell (21 August 1913).

Chapter 4: Return to the Old Country –WWI

1. Laffaye, 'Lewis Lacey', cited courtesy of L. A. Lacey Esq.

2. Hodder, *Activities of the British Community in Argentina during the Great War 1914–1919*, 25.

3. Ibid., 217.

4. Ibid., 218.

5. Peel, *The Polar Bear Hunt*, 28.

6. Graves, *Goodbye to All That*, 187.

7. John Campbell, letter to Dorothy Campbell (10 October 1916).

8. John Campbell, letter to Dorothy Campbell (15 November 1916).

9. National Museum of the Royal Navy, 'Biography: Captain Laurence Oates', <http://www.royalnavalmuseum.org/info_sheets_lawrence_oates.htm>, accessed March 2014.

10. *Standard* (Buenos Aires, 27 January 1917).

11. 'Telefonia', *Standard* (Buenos Aires, 28 January 1917).

12. *Standard* (Buenos Aires, 4 March 1917).

13. *Buenos Aires Herald* (9 March 1917).

14. John Campbell, grandson of J.A. Campbell, email to John Daffurn (23 April 2012).

15. 'War Diaries. 6 Inniskilling Dragoons', The National Archives (TNA), WO 95/1160/4.

16. 'Operations Carried out by the Mhow Cavalry Brigade on December 1st, 1917', *The Cavalry Journal*, 18 (1928), 48.

17. 'Long Service Papers. Lieutenant John Argentine CAMPBELL. Dragoon Guards', The National Archives (TNA), WO 339/45758.

18. Ibid.

19. Ibid.

20. Ibid.

Chapter 5: Jock's Demise

1. Graves, *Goodbye to All That*, 224.

2. Manz, 'Management Transfer in the Textile Industry: Otto Ernst Philippi at J. & P. Coats, 1878–1917', in S. Manz, J. Davis and M. S. Beerbühl, eds, *Migration and Transfer from Germany to Britain, 1660 to 1914: Historical Relations and Comparisons*, 171.

3. E. Philippi, 'A Loyal Naturalized British Subject's Views of the War', *Hampshire Chronicle and General Advertiser* (22 May 1915).

4. R. Philippi, private chronicle of the Philippi family.

5. Manz, 'Management Transfer', 171.

6. John Campbell, letter to Dorothy Campbell (23 March 1920).

7. Escribano Wilde, 'Campbell, Juan: Hipoteca a Shipton, Stewart', (28 June 1920), Archivo General de la Provincia de Tucuman, Protocolo Serie J, Tomo 1, Volumen 24, foja 368.

8. Dorothy Campbell, undated family history notes.

9. Tomás Chevallier-Boutell, 'Federal Countries', 5, citing Daniel J. Greenberg, *Sugar Depression and Agrarian Revolt* (Durham NC, 1987), <www.dundee.ac.uk/cepmlp/gateway/files.php?file=CAR-12_44...pdf>, accessed July 2014.

10. Peel, *The Polar Bear Hunt*, 42.

11. Colin Gale, Archives and Museum, Bethlem Royal Hospital, email to John Daffurn (9 January 2012).

Chapter 6: Like Father, Like Son – WWII

1. Margrit Philippi, photograph sent to Isabel Campbell (1 July 1939).

2. Lt Roderick Campbell, 'Army Service Personnel Record', Ministry of Defence, Glasgow.

3. Ibid.

4. Ibid.

5. Smith, 'Bletchley Park and the Holocaust', in L. V. Scott and P. D. Jackson, eds, *Understanding Intelligence in the Twenty-First Century*, 119.

6. 'War Diaries. 2/6 Queen's Royal Regiment (West Surrey)', The National Archives (TNA), WO 170/1466.

7. Ibid.

8. Michael Campbell, letter to Dorothy Campbell (3 October 1944).

Chapter 7: Heir-Hunting

1. Major R. M. Campbell MC, 'Army Service Personnel Record', Ministry of Defence, Glasgow.

Chapter 8: Isabel

1. 'Chelmsford Uber Alles', *Private Eye* (2 November 1973), 21.

2. Ibid.

3. Ibid.

4. Teacher, *Rogue Agents: Habsburg, Pinay and the Private Cold War 1951–1991*, Kindle location 3893.

5. Ibid., location 4954.

Select Bibliography

Anderson, W., *The Scottish Nation*, Vol. III (Edinburgh, 1863)

Archetti, Eduardo, P., *Masculinities: Football, Polo and the Tango in Argentina* (Oxford, 1999)

Bath, Richard, *The Scotland Rugby Miscellany* (London, 2007)

Bernardez, M., *The Argentine Estancia. A Review of the Livestock and Agricultural Industries of the Argentine Republic* (Buenos Aires, 1903)

Bletz, May E., *Immigration and Acculturation in Brazil and Argentina: 1890–1929* (New York, 2010)

Burn Murdoch, W. G., *Modern Whaling and Bear Hunting* (Philadelphia, 1917)

Cage, R. A., *The Scots Abroad: Labour, Capital, Enterprise, 1750–1914* (London, c. 1985)

Chamosa, Oscar, *The Argentine Folklore Movement: Sugar Elites, Criollo Workers, and the Politics of Cultural Nationalism, 1900–1955* (Tucson, c. 2010)

Darbyshire, Charles, *My Life in the Argentine Republic, etc.* (New York, 1918)

Dodds, J., *Records of the Scottish Settlers in the River Plate, and their Churches* (Buenos Aires, 1897)

Dreier, Katherine Sophie, *Five Months in the Argentine from a Woman's Point of View, 1918 to 1919* (New York, 1920)

Edwards, Todd L., *Argentina: A Global Studies Handbook* (Oxford, c. 2008)

Fernández-Gómez, Emilio Manuel. *Estancias y estancieros de barracas hasta el salado : la epopeya de los pioneros Británicos en el Campo Argentino* (Buenos Aires, 2004)

Fraser, John Foster, *The Amazing Argentine* (New York, 1914)

Gibbs, Philip, *The Battles of the Somme* (London, 1917)

Gibson, Herbert, *The History and Present State of the Sheep-Breeding Industry in the Argentine Republic* (Buenos Aires, 1893)

Graham-Yooll, A., *The Forgotten Colony: A History of the English-Speaking Communities in Argentina* (London, 1981)

Graves, Robert, *Goodbye to All That* (London, 1929, reprinted 2000)

Grierson, William, 'The Voyage of the *Symmetry*' in Iain A. D. Stewart, ed., *From Caledonia to the Pampas: Two Accounts by Early Scottish Emigrants to the Argentine* (Edinburgh, 2000)

Hammerton, J. A., *The Real Argentine: Notes and Impressions of a Year in the Argentine and Uruguay* (New York, 1916)

Hanon, Maxine, *Diccionario de británicos en Buenos Aires : primera época* (Buenos Aires, 2005)

Harper, Marjory, *Adventurers and Exiles* (London, 2003)

Hodder, Arthur, L., ed., *Activities of the British Community in Argentina during the Great War 1914–1919* (Buenos Aires, 1920)

Hora, Roy, *The Landowners of the Argentine Pampas: A Social and Political History, 1860–1945* (Oxford, 2001)

Hubback, J. H., *Life in Argentina* (Liverpool, 1908)

Hudson, W. H., *Far Away and Long Ago* (New York, 1918)

Hutchinson, Thomas Joseph, *Buenos Ayres and Argentine Gleanings: With Extracts from a Diary of Salado Exploration in 1862 and 1863* (London, 1865)

Jefferson, Mark Sylvester William, *Peopling the Argentine Pampa* (New York, 1926)

Koebel, W. H., *Argentina Past and Present* (Buenos Aires, 1910)

Laffaye, H. A., 'Lewis Lacey: Master of the Game' in H. A. Laffaye, ed., *Profiles in Polo: The Players who Changed the Game* (Jefferson, NC, 2007)

Laffaye, H. A., *The Evolution of Polo* (Jefferson, NC, 2009)

Larden, Walter, *Estancia Life: Agricultural, Economic, and Cultural Aspects of Argentine Farming* (London, 1911)

Love, George Thomas, *A Five Years Residence in Buenos Ayres, during the Years 1820 to 1825 ... by an Englishman* (London, 1825)

Lubbock, B., *The Colonial Clippers* (Glasgow, 1921)

McClure, G. W., '1891–1896' in H. R. Pyatt, ed., *Fifty Years of Fettes: Memories of Old* (Edinburgh, 1931)

Manz, Stefan, 'Management Transfer in the Textile Industry: Otto Ernst Philippi at J. & P. Coats, 1878–1917' in S. Manz, J. Davis, and M. S. Beerbühl, eds, *Migration and Transfer from Germany to Britain, 1660 to 1914: Historical Relations and Comparisons*, (München, 2007)

Masefield, John, *The Battle of the Somme* (London, 1919)

Moncrieff, A. R. Hope, *The Pampas; A Story of Adventure in the Argentine Republic* (London, 1876)

Mulhall, M. G. & Mulhall, E. T., *Handbook of the River Plate* (Buenos Ayres, 1869)

Norman, Terry, *The Hell they called High Wood: The Somme* (Wellingborough, 1989)

Ogilvie, P. Campbell, *Argentina from a British Point of View, and Notes on Argentine Life* (London, 1910)

Parish, Woodbine, *Buenos Ayres and the Provinces of the Rio de la Plata: From their Discovery and Conquest by the Spaniards to the Establishment of their Political Independence* (London, 1852)

Pastor, José Manuel Azcona, *Possible Paradises: Basque Emigration to Latin America* (Reno, Nevada, c. 2004)

Peel, C. V. A., *The Polar Bear Hunt* (London, 1928)

Poliakov, L., *The History of Anti-Semitism: From Voltaire to Wagner* (Philadelphia, 2003)

Pyatt, H. R., ed., *Fifty Years of Fettes: Memories of Old* (Edinburgh, 1931)

Rauch, George V., *Conflict in the Southern Cone: The Argentine Military and the Boundary Dispute with Chile, 1870–1902* (Westport, 1999)

Reber, Vera Blinn, *British Mercantile Houses in Buenos Aires, 1810–1880* (London, 1979)

Repington, Lt.-Col. Charles à Court, *The First World War, 1914–18* (London, 1920)

Robson, Jane, 'Faith Hard Tried: The Memoirs of Jane Robson' in Iain A. D. Stewart, ed., *From Caledonia to the Pampas: Two Accounts by Early Scottish Emigrants to the Argentine* (Edinburgh, 2000)

Rock, David, *Argentina, 1516–1987: From Spanish Colonization to Alfonsín* (Berkeley, 1987)

Seymour, Richard Arthur, *Pioneers in the Pampas, or, the First Four Years of a Settlers Experience in the La Plata Camps* (London, 1869)

Shaw, Arthur E., *Forty Years in the Argentine Republic* (Buenos Aires, 1907)

Smith, Michael, 'Bletchley Park and the Holocaust', in L. V. Scott and P. D. Jackson, eds, *Understanding Intelligence in the Twenty-First Century* (London, 2004)

Stevenson, J. A., '1896–1902' in H. R. Pyatt, ed., *Fifty Years of Fettes: Memories of Old* (Edinburgh, 1931)

Teacher, David, *Rogue Agents: Habsburg, Pinay and the Private Cold War 1951–1991* (Hastings, 2013)

Walter, Richard J., *Politics and Urban Growth in Buenos Aires, 1910–1942* (Cambridge, 1993)

Index